# Beyond the Comfort Zone

## Confessions of an Extreme Sports Junkie

_Bruce Gereveaux_

# Beyond the Comfort Zone

## Confessions of an Extreme Sports Junkie

**Whitewater Kayaking**

**Adventure Racing**

**Extreme Skiing**

**Rock Climbing**

Bruce Genereaux

CLASS FIVE PRESS
Hanover, New Hampshire

Published by: CLASS FIVE PRESS, Hanover, New Hampshire

First paper printing, December 2002

**Front Cover Image:** © 1998 by Catherine Hansford. Paddler: Jason Hansford. Location: Dry Meadow Creek, California
**Back Cover Images:** Author (1,3 & 4). Climber in 3 is Dave Suleski, Torrey Carroll (2). Paddler: Todd Dickson
**Cover Design:** Lynne Walker Design Studio. Hanover, New Hampshire
**Maps:** Peter C. Allen. Fairlee, Vermont
**Editing:** Freestyle Creative, Dena Foltz. Whitefish, Montana
**Printing:** Stinehour Press. Lunenburg, Vermont

*Library of Congress Cataloging-in-Publication Data*
Genereaux, Bruce M.
Beyond the comfort zone: confessions of an extreme sports junkie—whitewater kayaking, adventure racing, extreme skiing, rock climbing / by Bruce M. Genereaux. 220p. 2.0 cm.
Includes photos, drawings and index.
ISBN 0-9725173-2-4 (pbk.)

1. Adventure Narrative. 2. Extreme Sports. 3. Outdoor Recreation. 4. Kayaking.
5. Rock Climbing. 6. Adventure Racing. 7. Alpine Skiing. 8. Ski Racing.
9. Genereaux, Bruce M., 1963– Biography. I. Title
CIP tba

*Time, and unconditional love and support from my family have made this work possible*


*And to my dust-covered climbing and kayaking gear: your time may come again in the later stages of the "domestic adventure race"*

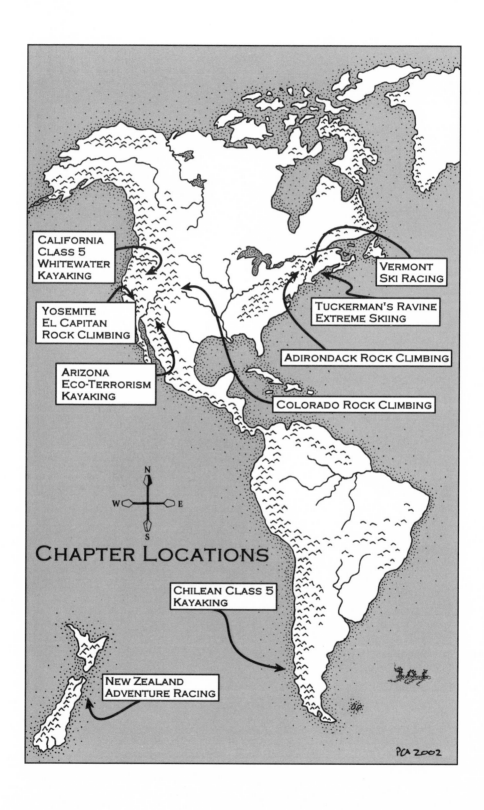

CHAPTER LOCATIONS

CALIFORNIA
CLASS 5
WHITEWATER
KAYAKING

YOSEMITE
EL CAPITAN
ROCK CLIMBING

ARIZONA
ECO-TERRORISM
KAYAKING

VERMONT
SKI RACING

TUCKERMAN'S RAVINE
EXTREME SKIING

ADIRONDACK ROCK CLIMBING

COLORADO ROCK CLIMBING

CHILEAN CLASS 5
KAYAKING

NEW ZEALAND
ADVENTURE RACING

N
W      E
S

PCA 2002

# Contents

The *Aiguille de Josh*, Joshua Tree National Park, California, April 1994. The author's bully pulpit moves from rock to paper with the publication of this book.

# Introduction

*Beyond the Comfort Zone* is an autobiographical adventure narrative that tells what it's like to extreme ski, rock climb, whitewater kayak and adventure race.

In each of these activities, I have pushed the limits of risk to extremes few people ever imagine, much less experience. I have been close to death more times than I like to admit, but admit them I do. The stories in this book are brutally honest. Each one transports a reader through intriguing worlds of difficult challenges, intensely hard work, stupid mistakes and laudable achievements.

Exploring beyond my comfort zone has been instinctive for me since I was a child. A predilection toward high risk behavior is surely programmed in my genes; but just as surely, it is a gift I was given by, amongst others, my paternal grandfather, Raymond Genereaux. He inspired and encouraged me with stories of his youth. His successes bolstered my confidence and gave me assurance that the ability to succeed was in my blood.

He told me of climbing Mt. St. Helens in 1917 when he was 15 years old. When I reported my ascent to him in 1986, five years after it erupted, his pride was evident, but he reminded me, part in jest, part in boast, that it was 1,300 feet higher when he summited. It was my grandfather who encouraged me to document my climbs and to be proud of victories won. I have kept a "recreational curriculum vita" for many years. This book came to fruition in part because of his prompt.

In 1999, five months before my grandfather's death, I dedicated my participation in a New Zealand adventure race to him because I wished to honor the direction he gave my life. The final chapter of this book tells the story of this race.

*Bruce M. Genereaux,*
Hanover, New Hampshire
November 2002

Chris Van Curan

**THE AUTHOR TAKES THE BAIT AT THE TOP OF LEFT GULLY IN MT. WASHINGTON'S TUCKERMAN'S RAVINE. APRIL 25, 1975.**

# Tuckerman's Ravine

*"The hook and treasure of a lifetime."*
—Chris Van Curan

## FIRST RISK

MY PARENTS RAISED ME IN A SUPPORTIVE ENVIRONMENT STEEPED IN SPORTS. FROM SAILING AND TENNIS, TO WILDERNESS HIKING CAMPS AND SKI RACING, I WAS EXPOSED TO COMPETITION AND NATURAL ELEMENTS SUCH THAT I CAME TO LOVE THE OUTDOORS AND ACCEPT ADVERSE CONDITIONS AS NORMAL.

MY FATHER AND HIS BUSINESS ASSOCIATE, CHRIS VANCURAN, SHARED A LOVE FOR THE MOUNTAINS OF NEW ENGLAND AND SKIING. AS OFTEN AS POSSIBLE, MY DAD AND CHRIS ESCAPED TO THEIR VERMONT AND NEW HAMPSHIRE SKI CHALETS FROM THEIR BANKING BUSINESSES IN NEW YORK AND BOSTON. IN THE SPRING OF 1975, WHEN I WAS 11 YEARS OLD, CHRIS AND MY DAD PLANNED TO INTRODUCE ME AND MY BROTHER TO NEW HAMPSHIRE'S TUCKERMAN'S RAVINE.

Brooks Dodge, Pinkham Notch's weatherman had forecast a "50 cent day"— top of the scale—clear, calm and relatively warm for April in northern New Hampshire. Since it was a Friday, we would have Tuckerman's Ravine to ourselves—perfect conditions for first-timers. My brother and I carried rucksacks in which our ski boots and sweaters were stuffed. My dad hefted a huge pack to his back. Three pair of skis jutted over his head like pickets on a fence.

"Try to step in my boot prints," Chris VanCuran instructed my brother and me as we hiked the snow-covered Fire Trail from Pinkham Notch to Tuckerman's Ravine. Chris was trying to make our first time up easy. While struggling to keep up on the hike, my thoughts drifted back to my father's description of Tuckerman's.

---

"The ravine is a glacial cirque. The center is called the headwall. The snow drifts 50 feet deep in the winter. The ravine has ice cliffs and rocks half way up, but you ski between them," my dad had said.

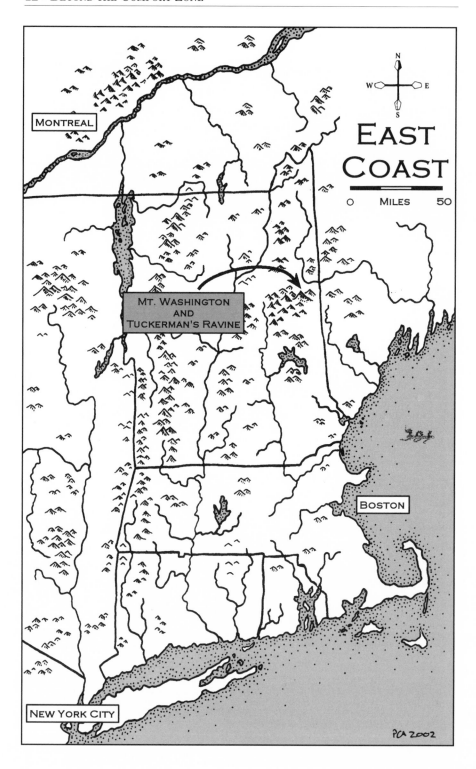

"How tall is it?" I had asked, leaning over the front seat as we drove north from New York.

"About half as tall as the Empire State Building," he replied.

I tried to picture it, but could not imagine what it would really be like. All I thought about was how exciting it would be to do something that my dad said very few people were good enough skiers to do.

My mom told us to be careful as we left, a sign that skiing the ravine might be risky. Dad and mom climbed up to Tuckerman's Ravine in 1960. Few people then even considered skiing it. It was my dad's Holy Grail and now he was going to get a chance to share it with his sons. His enthusiasm was infectious.

"It's so steep—about 45- to 55-degrees—that you can't see the slope from the top," he said. Our parents had taken us skiing and to ski races all over the East since we were four. Dad believed we could tackle whatever Tuckerman's might offer.

---

After two hours of hiking, we rested on the deck of HoJo's, the caretaker's shelter, and caught our first glimpse of the infamous ravine. It loomed above like a white drape speckled and bound by rocks, ice and dark cliffs. It was so vast that it filled the whole view to the west.

We continued along the trail, skirting house-sized boulders and emerged from treeline where soaring chutes, walls of snow and icebound cliffs were revealed. My pulse quickened and we eschewed any warm up run, determined to head all the way to the top for our first run. My brother and I shouldered our skis and followed Chris up the Left Gully. Each step he kicked was the equivalent of two of mine. The base of the gully started out as steep as the hardest expert trail I knew. Looking upward, the snow loomed progressively steeper. Dark cliffs jutted from the edges of the gully to my left and right only fifty feet apart. I felt like I was inside the mountain.

I methodically climbed upward. My brother stopped to put his skis on just below the near-vertical face of the final cornice, which looked impossible to surmount.

"Just above it flattens out," Chris said.

The slope was so steep that, while standing upright, the snow grazed the fingertips of my outstretched arm—a relationship that drove home the steepness of the gully. Even greater difficulty loomed in the form of the final cornice. I wanted to find out what was beyond the cornice and go as high as I could. Even at age eleven, I couldn't resist taking a risk just to see where it would take me.

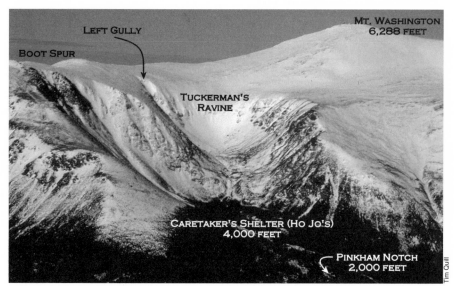

LEFT GULLY

BOOT SPUR

MT. WASHINGTON
6,288 FEET

TUCKERMAN'S
RAVINE

CARETAKER'S SHELTER (HO JO'S)
4,000 FEET

PINKHAM NOTCH
2,000 FEET

**EAST FACE OF MT. WASHINGTON, WHITE MOUNTAINS, NEW HAMPSHIRE.**

I swung my skis to the side to keep the tips from digging in. Using my free hand, I reached into each step and dug my fingers down and in, creating a handhold onto which I latched. Once I started, I realized I was committed. Twenty gut-clenching steps later, the slope abruptly flattened, revealing the broad shoulder of Boot Spur. My pulse slowed.

I looked down to where we started that morning three thousand feet below and two miles distant. The road was a long way away, but I wasn't worried. Above, the summit of Mt. Washington was draped in bright, smooth snowfields. For a boy used to the confines of the treed trails found at Eastern ski areas, this open expanse of skiable terrain was bigger than any I had imagined. It was like a dream come true. I felt like the curtains were drawn back and a window was opened on new worlds of opportunity my athletic abilities might bring me.

"Put 'em on here and traverse that way," Chris instructed.

I traversed to the edge of the corniced gully. My tips edged over the lip, from which the mountain seemed to fall straight down. No wonder the hike up was scary. The gully was far steeper than anything I had ever skied. I didn't even wait for Chris to lead, I plunged ahead.

The snow was smooth, textbook corn snow. Each turn was effortless. I went from cliff edge to cliff edge, putting up a spray like a waterskier with each turn. As the gully flattened out I took a beeline to where my dad waited. I was elated. I had received a perfect reward for pushing my comfort zone on the hike up.

Tuckerman's had set its hook that day, starting me on a lifetime of adventure.

TWENTY YEARS LATER, THE AUTHOR STILL
HAS THE HOOK IN HIS MOUTH. HERE HE DE-
SCENDS *SHIT-FOR-BRAINS* COULOIR ADJA-
CENT TO ARAPAHOE BASIN SKI AREA IN
COLORADO.

AT THE 1986 NCAA DIVISION I NATIONAL CHAMPIONSHIPS AT MT. MANSFIELD SKI AREA IN STOWE, VERMONT, THE AUTHOR APPROACHES THE EDGE OF HIS COMFORT ZONE.

# Ski Racing

## ALL AMERICAN REGRET

I stood in the start house, ski tips quivering, poles firmly planted over the timing wand, ready to make my final run in the giant slalom as a member of the Middlebury College Division I ski team. Classmates, parents and other spectators stood shoulder to shoulder along the course below.

The PA system bellowed, "Next on course: Racer number 16, Bruce Genereaux of Middlebury College." Cheers rose up. The nervousness in my belly exceeded any I had felt before.

I rocked my weight back, body cocked. The starter leaned close, "Five seconds. Racer ready . . .Three, two, one, go!" I kick-started through the wand and attacked the course, skating and poling towards the first gate, trying to gain as much speed as possible. If I matched my first run's performance, I would become an *All American*, the highest honor in collegiate athletics.

It was my fourth year on the team. I was a giant slalom specialist, and if conditions were right I could be one of the fastest college racers on the hill. Earlier that year, at UVM's carnival at Stowe, I notched second place on one run, my best result to date—confirming my potential. However, it would take two runs at that standard to give an equivalent overall result—the only result that counted.

Alpine ski racing is similar to track and field sprints: hours of training culminating in a race lasting 60 to 90 seconds with mere hundredths of seconds separating finishers. Traveling at speeds up to 60 miles per hour, over bumps, through ruts and brushing inch-thick plastic gates, the slightest mistake could mean a crash or seconds lost. Style did not matter, only speed.

Over a season there were a series of carnivals, the name given northeastern US college Division I ski races—at Bates College, St. Lawrence, University of New Hampshire, Dartmouth, University of Vermont, Williams and Middlebury—all capped off by a national competition that included Western schools. The NCAA national

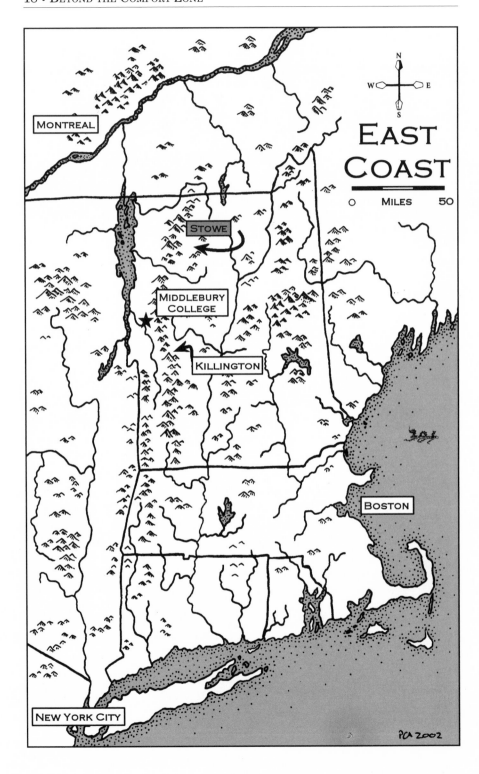

championships doubled the density of talent in the race. Hours of on- and off-snow preparation, coaching, training, ski waxing and van time prepared me for 30 minutes per year of actual competition. While this ratio of preparation to competition implied what I deemed a game of "hurry up and wait," when it was my turn to pit myself against the mountain and fellow competitors, I experienced unrivaled exhilaration during those seconds.

While racing, I realized a primal, almost visceral, distraction-free period in which I tried to conquer fear of crashing or injury, push myself to the limit and seek the perfect turn. Finding the right balance of these elements brought me satisfaction. No sport I knew matched the thrill of charging down a steep, icy mountain at speeds up to 60 miles per hour.

My preparation for this final season started 15 years before at Killington. My parents bought equipment, helped officiate in freezing temperatures and drove hours each weekend to support my passion.

By the end of high school, I was ranked the 50th best giant slalom racer in the country. My parents agreed to support a one-year, make or break, post-high school academic hiatus to try for the US Ski Team and, hopefully, the Olympics. I went north to Burke Mountain Academy in Vermont where I expanded my physical comfort zone regularly, but failed to make the next plateau of ski racing.

Fortunately, my academics had not been neglected and I shifted my focus to a liberal arts education and college ski racing at Middlebury. During each winter season, my academic and social priorities often took a back-seat to my sport. I was driven to maintain a ranking on one of the most prestigious teams on a campus where sports are highly regarded.

College ski racing is a team event, yet, like many timed sports, its highest honor recognizes individual success. This linkage yielded a conflict for me. If I sought only individual honor, I encountered a unique aspect of ski racing: the faster I went, and the more chances I took to gain speed, the more likely I would fall and get no result, thus hurting the team. Alternatively, backing off too much and getting consistently poorer results would also erode my position on the team, an untenable option for someone naturally competitive and whose self-esteem was bolstered by team membership.

My talent was such that I could come close to winning in the giant slalom if I was aggressive and bold. But in reality I was not sufficiently talented to do this with any margin of security. For me to win, I had to take chances which often meant falling. Thus I was often a top ten finisher, but seldom on the podium. My constant challenge was to discover how far I could push my limits and still be satisfied with the ultimate outcome.

Bob Perry

**THE AUTHOR TRAINING SLALOM AT KILLINGTON SKI AREA, 1970.**

This challenge is an issue addressed by many: Should one operate within his or her comfort zone or extend beyond it to achieve greatness at a higher risk of achieving nothing? Later in life, my behavior, in the context of this question, would nearly kill me.

Only three Middlebury racers (including me) had qualified for the All American race at Stowe. This was the same number of skiers who could score. A fall by any of our team's racers would mean no team score—a material blow to the team's chances in a tight overall competition.

By my senior year I had come to realize my mortality as a college ski racer. Jobs, graduate school and an unknown future were surely going to be much less glamorous than what I had been experiencing. But to leave a record—other than an essentially unrecorded contribution to generally fourth and fifth place national team results and my memories—became increasingly important. Vanity was invading my decision-making process.

Regardless of the increased chance of choking under my self-imposed pressure, on the first of two runs, I broke out of my mold and let it all hang out, taking risks and boldly attacking the course—chancing a fall and no result at all. I hadn't made a conscious decision to take the chances, it seemed to just happen, maybe because I felt comfortable with this same race hill on which, only a month before, I had had the second place result. I finished that run in seventh place, a mere five-tenths of a second behind the leader, my best first run result ever in a national competition. A top-ten result after two runs would put me on the All American team—an enviable cap to my ski racing career. Now I was not only in my last race, I had the chance for glory I had not fully imagined would come my way.

Before the second run was scheduled to start, I inspected the reset course. I rode the chairlift by myself, head spinning with the significance of my next run. I imagined my upcoming run.

*"Hold a low, aerodynamic position on the upper flats, working speed from every turn. Then, over the knoll and down the steep pitch, set up, ski rounder. Make sure you don't dump speed at the tight gates half way down the pitch."* My technical planning and expectations failed to allow me to slip into an intuitive psyche where I could let myself go like I had on the first run and allow my experience to guide me on the fastest line through the gates.

At the start I slipped into my normal pre-race concentration. Friends skied by, calling encouragement. I saw a glint in my coach's eye. The conflict between finishing with a conservative run for the team versus risking everything for higher individual achievement was all there in his look. I think he wanted me to do both somehow.

The first gates were easy. I carved clean arcs in the icy snow, accelerating with each turn. The trail turned, the gates shifted and I adjusted, staying aerodynamic over the bumps. I was carrying more speed than I thought I could—resulting in a welcome, but unnerving feeling. Ski racers are supposed to go fast, so fast that they might fall. I thought, *"Keep it up, keep it up."* I knew in my gut that I had crossed over the line between mediocrity and superiority. I saw the horizon line marking the knoll and couldn't see the next gates. I only remembered that the steep, tight section was coming fast. *"Don't blow it now. Remember to set up for the tight turns."*

At the first turn on the steeps I reverted to the technical plan I had formulated on the chairlift. First gate, no problem, second hard gate, no problem. I persisted in this round-line strategy, expecting that I'd feel on the edge of control like earlier in the course. But, all the gates stayed easy. I lost the element of risk that marks a fast run. I was suddenly well within my comfort zone, a place I did not want to be.

Desperate to recover from my mistake, I consciously switched tactics and took chances with a radically straight line through the final gates before the finish. Crossing the finish line, I saw my time was off the pace by two seconds—an eternity in a ski race. My heart sunk. It was too late to recover. Having made the investment, I failed to generate a return. I knew at this level of competition there was no quarter, no other top competitor had made my mistake. As the other competitors finished, my overall place slipped from sixth to 14th. My only consolation was that I was the fastest for Middlebury that day and the team's result was respectable as a result of my contribution. My team hat was proud, but my individual hat was inescapably disappointed.

Regret over not maximizing my personal results taints what was, in the big picture, a fine cap to a ski racing career. From that day forward I resolved to make the most of each chance I was given or could generate for myself.

THE 1986 MIDDLEBURY COLLEGE MEN'S ALPINE SKI TEAM. FROM LEFT, EBBE ALTBERG, PAT CALLAHAN, THE AUTHOR, JIM WEST AND STEVE PUTNAM

BRAD SCHILDT CONTEMPLATES THE PRICE OF IMPULSIVENESS ON THE SUM-MIT OF GIANT MOUNTAIN, 4,600 FEET, ADIRONDACK MOUNTAINS, NEW YORK.

# Giant Mountain's Eagle Slide

## A Brush with Death

The following story takes place in 1986 while I was a senior at Middlebury College.

Standing by itself at the north end of the Adirondack's High Peaks is 4,600-foot tall Giant Mountain. Though 60 miles distant and across Lake Champlain, it is a visible landmark from Middlebury College. On clear days it beckoned to serious climbers. The mountain's southern side, adorned by Eagle Slide, features a smooth, treeless rock face that was denuded by a massive landslide in the mid-1960s. Now kept clear by winter avalanches, the slide's rock is much like granite in texture, but greener, darker and glassier. Fourteen hundred feet long and 1,000 feet high, a climb up Eagle Slide was to be my first lead-climbing experience. I would share the experience with my friend and fraternity brother, Brad Schildt.

The previous fall and spring, Brad taught me to climb using a nearly risk-free method of climbing called top-roping, where we secured our rope to a cliff-top tree. On occasion we met more experienced climbers who told of climbs longer than one rope length. Their climbs were done from the bottom up using chocks and a series of belay ledges to advance the rope up the cliff. This technique and the environs in which it was used were the next step in our climbing development. We couldn't wait to try our hand, and Eagle Slide seemed a logical objective.

However, a few days before our intended outing, Brad and my relationship went off belay. Growing up, sometimes I had too much fun at others' expense and other times I damaged myself with my impulsiveness. Brad overindulged at a party and was "sleeping it off" on a couch in the fraternity. Four of us picked him up, each holding a limb, and carried him out the front door towards my waiting pickup truck. The plan was to drop him off somewhere else as a practical joke. Halfway to the truck he woke up, squirmed out of our grasp and stalked away.

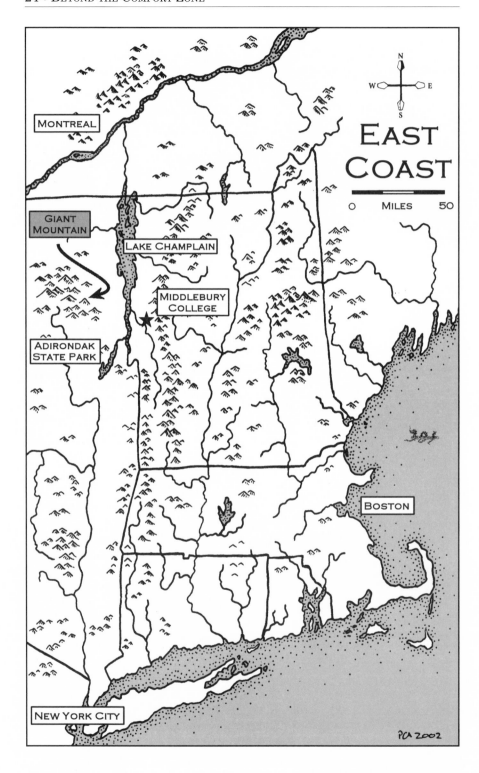

A few days later, Brad came into my room in the early hours of the morning while I was sleeping, put his hands on my neck and held me down to the bed. I squirmed, pushed and pulled, but failed to pry his hands from my neck. Finally, I got my legs into the fray and pushed him off.

In the silence of my empty room, I calmed down and thought things over. My introduction to rock climbing by Brad earlier that year had had a marked effect. What climbing lacked in the speed and fluidity of motion that made ski racing so rewarding was more than compensated by its demands of strength, smarts and ability to accept risk. My ski racing career was finished and I longed for the next activity through which I could define myself.

My passion for climbing's adventure and risk had strengthened Brad and my college friendship. Now a sophomoric prank had brought us to blows. I felt that more than an eye for an eye had been returned with his retaliation and resentment festered in me.

Graduation week should have been carefree—my thesis was defended and I had a job lined up. Because of my conflict with Brad, I had lost my regular climbing partner, and free time was running out. After graduation we would all scatter. My desire for adventure spurred me to capitulate. He and I voiced our differences and a day later we agreed to climb together again. Intending to rope up with someone whom I had just fought with was undoubtedly risky, but I couldn't resist the opportunity to do the climbs of which he spoke, particularly Eagle Slide.

We set out from campus at dawn. The weather was overcast and damp—conditions not normally suited for rock climbing. We intended to climb anyway, such was our unspoken drive to climb and my need to try such a climb before Brad and I went our separate ways. The approach took us up through a boulder-filled streambed to the base of the slide, where accumulated avalanche debris blocked us from starting right at its base. We climbed steadily up the vegetation along the right edge of the slide, looking anxiously for the logical spot to step out onto the slide. Finally, an obvious break in the bush revealed the start of my "dream climb." I was pumped.

From our vantage point, Eagle Slide appeared as a patchwork of damp moss and lichen on an expanse of rock the size of the flight deck of an aircraft carrier angled up 45 degrees. Grass and saplings grew from weaknesses in the rock. The bare rock was lightly dimpled like the peeled skin of a giant golf ball laid flat. There were no sharp edges or regular cracks for our feet or hands. I knew instinctively that climbing this smooth face unroped was risky. A rope would be the only thing that would save us from a fall. Yet, I acted contrarily to my observation.

"It doesn't look that steep," I commented. Both Brad and I had climbed snow steeper than this slide on our annual "rite-of-spring" pilgrimages to Tuckerman's Ravine on Mt. Washington.

"I'll go ahead till it feels like we should rope up and put our rock shoes on," said Brad.

"I'll be behind you," I said. Deferring to his experience, my mind impulsively focused on getting on the rock. Right away I could see that unroped climbing implied an even higher level of freedom than I imagined I would feel using the multi-rope length lead climbing technique. Being unroped appealed to me even more. Our encounter in my room still smarted. All I wanted to do was get climbing up the slide and I wasn't going to show any lack of certainty in front of Brad because it would be like salt in the wound of my resentment.

We started rock climbing 500 feet above the jumbled debris at the base of the slab. In his backpack was our rope and his harness and shoes. Brad moved out onto the face. I gave him room before moving out across the slab myself. He looked stable and was moving steadily. My sticky rock climbing shoes remained in my pack. "This is what I came for," I thought as I touched the rock for the first time.

Armed with brand new boots that I thought would help me climb, I traversed up and across the slab, pressing my boot soles into dimples and palming the smooth rock for balance. At first my feet felt secure in the stiff-soled boots. However, as I moved out and up, the soles started to either not fit or stick in the dimples. With one foot gripping the rock, there were times when I had to sample a few dimples before I found one that felt like it would hold my other foot.

When I next broke from my myopic search for foot holds and looked around, I saw I was over 100 feet from the treed edge of the slide. I tensed up, suddenly feeling like I'd driven into a snow corner too fast. A giant expanse of smooth slab now stretched between me and the debris at the base. No rope, no experience, no way to retreat, boots slipping and leg muscles tensed, I took a few more tenuous steps trying to gain secure footing.

When neither foot held in its dimple I started to slide backwards. Desperately trying to grip the rock as I slid faster and faster, my stomach tightened instinctively and I started to feel the first pangs of panic and fear.

Accelerating downwards, consequences flashed in my mind. I remembered nothing blocking my path to the rocky debris pile nearly 700 feet below. I realized the odds of surviving this fall were tiny.

I wasn't a goner yet. There was still enough friction between me and the sloping rock face to keep me from plunging out of control. I deliberately

GIANT MOUNTAIN
4,600 FEET

1,400 FEET

ACCIDENT SITE

Olaf Sööt

**GIANT MOUNTAIN'S SOUTH FACE. EAGLE SLIDE EXTENDS FROM THE LOWER CENTER TO THE TOP CENTER, IN THE SHAPE OF A BIRD IN FLIGHT. THE LINE OF ASCENT IS IMPOSED OVER THE IMAGE WITH THE ACCIDENT SITE CIRCLED.**

A CLIMBER ON EAGLE SLIDE WHO CHOOSES TO USE A ROPE. BLACK COATING ON ROCK AT RIGHT IS LICHEN.

flipped over onto my back, feet down, face out and saw the full scope of my upcoming fall. I felt like a beginner on an expert ski slope who had fallen and was now sliding faster and faster down the slope. My heart pounded in my throat.

Horizontal cracks in the slab rushed up toward me. The first crack did nothing to slow me. My feet skipped over it and my tailbone slammed into its edge. Pain shot up my spine. Next, a four-inch-wide crack rushed up. I reached for it with my heels. My feet dropped neatly into the crack only to be violently driven back towards me, slamming into my butt.

Just as I expected my heels to skip free, they snagged, tipping me forward and jouncing me up off the slab. I twisted quickly, thrusting my feet forward again, landing on my tailbone again.

Accelerating sharply now with no cracks to slow me, I skidded along— hands at my sides, feet out front. Most of my weight was on my butt, in hopes that dragging it would slow me down. I desperately tried to stay balanced and in control. I was now going too fast to attempt a repeat of the foot-in-crack trick. In seconds I would lose control, spin sideways and rag-doll all the way to the base. For the first time in my life I knew this loss of control could take on much higher consequences than any fraternity prank or chancy ski racing tactic.

My other rock climbing falls were caught by the rope so quickly I hardly had time to react or think of the consequences. This time my adrenaline surged while I swallowed the sickening feeling of dread and fought to survive.

Just ahead, I saw a small thicket of birch saplings growing from a car-sized recessed ledge. I reacted instinctively.

Ten feet before I reached the edge of this ledge, I pulled my legs up under me like a crab and pushed up with hands and feet at the same time. This ski racing-type "pre-jump" worked perfectly. It forced my trajectory initially up and then more steeply down into the recessed ledge instead of allowing me to sail over it.

Caboose first, arms outstretched, I hadn't slowed a bit when I landed halfway out the sapling-covered ledge. I bounced and tumbled, only partially slowed by the ledge's vegetation as I crashed through it. I flailed, my hands wide, clutching for any sapling. The one I did grab wrenched parallel to the rock face while my body kept right on going. But I held tight. My hand ripped up the sapling's narrowing trunk into the thinning branches at the top, and with my arm stretched tight, I came to a tenuous stop a few feet below the ledge.

After a moment's hesitation, I climbed, hand-over-hand, up the bent sapling to the ledge.

I removed my pack and sat down, stunned. My judgement had failed me. I chastised myself for not at least using the sticky rock shoes I had brought or sucking it up and asking Brad to break out the rope right away. I shuddered, realizing how close I had come to falling all the way to my death. My cavalier attitude towards the climb had been replaced with respect and the sinking "I told you so" feeling that accompanies a stupid mistake.

Brad moved to a nearby ledge, put on his harness and climbing shoes, placed a metal chock in a crack, tied off and lowered the rope down to me. I pressed my oozing hands to my shorts, trying to stop the stinging and bleeding. I squeezed back tears of anguish.

I laced up my climbing shoes. "On belay," I shouted after tying the rope to my harness. I never considered turning back, both for the practical reason of lack of knowledge as to how to rappel down such a face and because I knew Brad and I would climb by the book from now on. I was neither scared nor anxious about climbing on, just determined to do it right.

The security of the rope and climbing shoes made climbing up the ground over which I had just slid easy. I passed pieces of my shorts and flecks of skin on the rock as I ascended. I realized just how lucky I had been. The two cracks I passed were the only ones for hundreds of feet. I looked back at the sapling-covered ledge. It too was the only one and it was only ten feet wide.

We reached the summit uneventfully and found it socked in. Brad sat on one side of the clearing and I paced around the other, unable to sit. I was missing the normal charge I got from summiting a mountain or climb. My hands burned and oozed. My butt stung and my tailbone throbbed.

As we descended the mountain, I was self-absorbed. Stepping beyond my limit on campus and on Eagle Slide forced me, at least temporarily, to face the price of my impulsiveness.

DESPITE MY SOPHOMORIC BEHAVIOR OF THOSE DAYS, BRAD AND I CONTINUE TO CHALLENGE OURSELVES ON MOUNTAINS, CLIFFS AND RIVERS. HE RECENTLY BECAME GODFATHER TO MY SON.

Glenn Randall

THE SOUTH PLATTE REGION OF COLORADO IS KNOWN FOR ITS PINE FORESTS, GRANITE DOMES AND CLEAR, TROUT-FILLED RIVERS. ABOVE, BIG ROCK CANDY MOUNTAIN RISES 1,000 FEET ABOVE THE SOUTH PLATTE RIVER. THE ROUTE THE AUTHOR ATTEMPTED, *CHILDHOOD'S END*, ASCENDS THE CENTER BUTTRESS.

# Colorado's Big Rock Candy Mountain

## CHILDHOOD'S END

AFTER GRADUATE SCHOOL AT COLORADO SCHOOL OF MINES, MY PENT-UP DEMAND FOR CLIMBING EQUIPMENT AND BASIC LUXURIES WAS FILLED BY THE PAY I RECEIVED FROM THE JOB I TOOK IN DENVER WITH A FORTUNE 500 MINING COMPANY. I KEPT IN PEAK SHAPE DESPITE THIS 8-5 JOB BY BECOMING WHAT I CALLED A "WEEKNIGHT" CLIMBING AND MOUNTAIN BIKE WARRIOR, TRAINING FROM FIVE TO DARK EACH DAY. MY CLIMBING GOALS MOVED PROGRESSIVELY HIGHER AFTER EACH WEEKEND FORAY TO THE WEALTH OF CLIMBING ACCESSIBLE FROM DENVER. FOR YEARS I EYED THE LONGEST ROCK CLIMB IN COLORADO'S SOUTH PLATTE REGION, AN 11-PITCH ROUTE CALLED *CHILDHOOD'S END*. A NAME THAT, TO ME, IMPLIED A RITE-OF-PASSAGE. AS USUAL, WHEN I PUSHED TO NEW LEVELS, I GOT MORE THAN I BARGAINED FOR.

My four-wheel drive car skidded and growled down granite slabs and through deep gravel as we descended into Wildcat Canyon—an enchanted wilderness along the South Platte River, two hours south of Denver. Our objective, Big Rock Candy Mountain, was hidden on the other side of the river.

I spied a place where other vehicles had forded. I thought little of the consequences of a river crossing. "This rig can make it across a river like that, lets go for it," I said to my climbing partner, Rob, a former college classmate and industry colleague. Low range engaged, we plunged down the embankment into the river, hoping to glimpse our climb.

The South Platte River drains the continental divide. Its water is cold, deep and unforgiving. Halfway across the river and 50 feet from the far bank, we stalled and lurched to a stop. The beautiful "bow" wave in front of the grill continued on without us. We sat in silence punctuated only by the pinging of the cooling engine and the hiss of steam. The water lapped at headlight level. I reached out the window and touched the water. I looked down at my feet and saw water pooling.

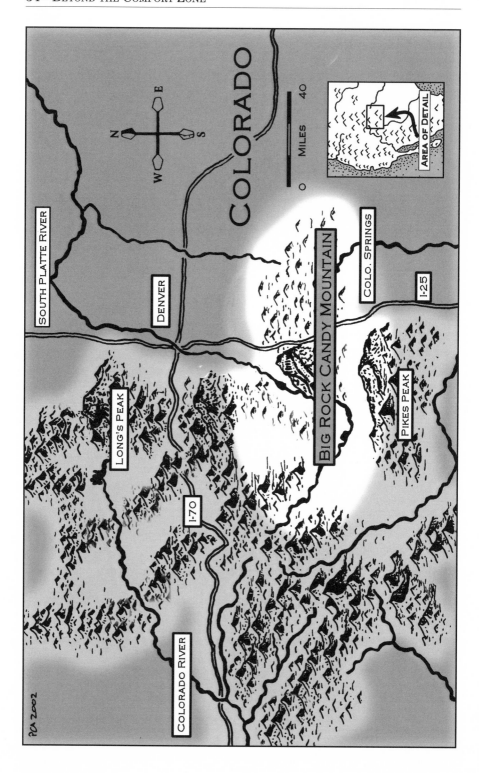

We could probably convince fishermen we had seen down river to pull us out. But, if we used our climbing rope as a tow rope, our climb would be shot. We could walk 15 miles to the nearest house and call a tow truck. But that cost might set me back to my bean burrito graduate school diet. Regardless, my impulsiveness was having an immediate effect: loss of vehicular freedom and a wasted opportunity to test myself on Big Rock Candy Mountain.

We discussed the effect of frigid river water on electrical systems and hot engine blocks. Was it the resistance of water on the cooling fan? Or was it the high back pressure on the exhaust system?

On the chance that none of the reasons we discussed caused the stall, I tried to restart the engine. After what seemed like minutes of the starter motor whining and the cooling fan churning water like a stern wheeler, the engine sputtered, coughed and stuttered to life. Amazed at my luck, I coaxed the RPMs higher and higher, spewing frothing, aerated water from under the hood. I threw in the clutch, popped it into first and burned river gravel till we hit dry land.

Lurching to a stop in the grass on the far side of the river, Rob said, "Bruce, look there it is." Big Rock Candy Mountain was clearly visible now, back on the side we had just come from.

**INTERIOR FLOODING, BRUISED EGOS, A FAILED WEEKEND ADVENTURE, AN EX-ORBITANTLY COSTLY TOW AND POSSIBLY A RUINED ENGINE CAN RESULT FROM PRESUMING YOUR FOUR-WHEEL DRIVE RIG IS AMPHIBIOUS.**

"No way am I going back across, we have to get out on this side," I said. The novelty of the river crossing had almost immediately worn off. Having an operating car to get me to work was rationale enough to defer our attempt on *Childhood's End* till another day.

"I don't see any roads," Rob said.

"The map shows one on top of that hill. I'm going to try to go up through the woods," I said, preparing to do battle with the environment by putting fresh tracks across a pristine forest floor.

No matter how fast a running start I got before the hill, we ground to a halt. I started to feel badly about the damage I was doing to the hillside. My spirits sagged as I reluctantly came to the conclusion that fording the river again was my only salvage option. Rob waded down river a bit and found a shallower crossing spot. This time we crossed without incident.

Now oriented, we drove down the river to a cul-de-sac camping area near the base of the climb. While unwinding over dinner after our brush with the river gods, we set our sights on our intended route, *Childhood's End*. At 1,300 feet long and 1,000 feet high, *Childhood's End* was the longest rock climb in Colorado's Front Range outside of Rocky Mountain National Park. I viewed it as a chance to test how much my climbing had improved.

Routes in the South Platte region are established at high ethical standards, i.e.,: ground to cliff top using only natural features. Any bolts added for safe ascent are placed from natural stances. Style mattered to the first ascensionists.

I viewed those who had first climbed these remote granite domes as almost mythical creatures. For their first ascents required bodies and minds as hard as steel. I had first learned about Big Rock Candy Mountain in Glenn Randall's 1984 book, *Vertigo Games*, a classic visual and written portrait of Colorado climbing and its pioneers. Then, only a few weeks before my attempt on Big Rock Candy Mountain, I actually met Pete Williams, the first ascensionist I had read about in Randall's book. He made BRCM sound easy. I aspired to his perspective.

Tucked tight in my mummy bag, I lay wondering if I was up to the next day's challenge. Rob was nearby, comfortably perched on his MPL (Multi-Position Lounger—$7.99 at your local discount store)—a poor man's cot. I drifted off with my fear of the uncertainty of the next day's adventure manifesting itself as a slight shudder through my chest—like I'd just finished crying.

Loud sniffing at my head and a waft of foul breath woke me from my childhood-ending dreams. I sat bolt upright and screamed. The animal source of the sniffing turned tail with deep hackle-raising guttural fear-yelps and ran into the woods. Rob, hearing my feral screams, tried to scramble to my defense, but, entangled in his mummy bag, got folded up in his MPL and was unceremoniously ejected onto the ground.

Being east coast, liberal arts-educated lads, guns did not make the car-camping gear checklist, however our thoughts over the next half hour edged towards a more *"Live Free or Die"* philosophy. The sound of the howling and size of the animal convinced us we were up against some kind of large canine, maybe even a wolf (despite the fact that we well knew the last of the wolves had gone to the happy hunting ground along with most of the buffalo in Colorado). We talked of posting watches. Finally the "wolf" stopped its howling and pacing. We rested fitfully.

In the morning light we measured paw prints in excess of four inches across. My mood swung from the uncertainty that the "wolf" added to my climb-anticipation fears to confidence gained from knowing now that I had scared off a beast of considerable size who was obviously evaluating easy prey.

Egos full from foiling attack, we made the easy approach to the foot of the climb. So far luck had allowed us to best a river and a wolf. Now it was time to literally address the metaphoric *Childhood's End* route. I doubted luck would have much to do with being able to climb the longest and hardest climb I had faced yet.

From our vantage at the base of the cliff, the beginning of the route didn't actually look that steep. Rob, in his anxiousness to begin, climbed straight up through the initially easy moves—foregoing the route described in our guidebook because the direct line looked easy. Spending nearly all of his physical and mental savings gingerly buying foot after foot of progress, he moved along minute depressions and finger-sized ledges, all the while growing increasingly distant from his last protection point.

At 80 feet off the deck I called up, "You're looking at a ground fall now." At that moment, it no longer seemed that knocking off *Childhood's End* would be that easy. After whimpers and machinations about the lack of protection, Rob continued upwards, completing the last friction mantle to the belay ledge with an audible breath of relief.

The next six pitches, while easier than our direct start on the first, got progressively harder. The rock on these pitches was characterized by half-inch crystals protruding from a 65-degree slab. There were three to five bolts per 100- to 150-foot pitch. The consequence of a fall would be a 60-foot tumble and slide before Rob could catch me with the rope. The possibility of a fall sharpened my senses and made me conscious of each step, but didn't overshadow the experience. I loved being up high on the cliff, looking down at the river, feeling the wind in my hair and the sun on my shoulders.

As we turned the corner on pitch seven, we encountered a section of rock so steep and smooth and devoid of protection that there was no way I could proceed. So, we broke out our "cheater" stick, an elongated tent pole with a carabiner on its end. Designed for surmounting "too-hard-for-me" sections, we used it to aid through this 5.12[1] difficulty "crux" pitch. I believed the first ascensionists would never have used such a style, but our lack of ability led to a "success over style" ethic. What shook me was the fact that another human being could possibly climb such a section without assistance. I had a long way to go as a climber if I was to be good enough to pioneer a similar route.

After the lead, I waited, suspended by nylon slings on the nearly-vertical, smooth face held by carabiners clipped to two quarter-inch bolts adorned with rusty hangers, while Rob jümared[2] up. It was here, 700 feet above the river, that I began to appreciate how committed I was to this climb. Below was a nearly-smooth apron of rock that curled downward out of sight, revealing only the meandering river backdrop. My inability to see the connection between what I rested on and the ground was unnerving. Two rusty bolt hangers that flexed with each of Rob's jümar steps were all that held us. I willed myself to relax and accept the queasiness of seeing the metal fatiguing before my eyes. This and the unsettling feeling of disassociation from the ground were part of the price of upward progress.

Contrary to the view of the flexing metal attached to the rock, the view outward from my tenuous perch was soothing. I saw typical South Platte scenery—evergreen trees spread out below like ocean waves from which domes called Sheepshead, Wigwam and Sunshine surfaced and through which the river carved a meandering and sometimes tumultuous passage. I looked above and saw the candy-striped section of Big Rock Candy Mountain up close for the first time. There, four-foot-wide water grooves, smooth except for half-inch protruding crystals, descended ever-steepening down 600 feet from the summit. My sweet tooth for adventure pulled me upward.

---

1. Rock climbing difficulty ratings range from Class 1 through 5. Within Class 5 (rope required to arrest fall) subdivisions from 5.0 (easiest) to 5.9 grade subjectively harder climbs. Mathematically illogical gradings of 5.10, 5.11 up to 5.15 (as of 2002) complete today's scale. BRCM's lower pitches rate between 5.7 and 5.12. Its final three pitches are rated 5.5 and 5.6.

Aid climbing is when pre-placed pitons or other protection devices are used to assist in climbing sections of the cliff that lack natural hand and foot holds.

2. A means of ascending just the rope with mechanical one-way devices.

3 RUN-OUT PITCHES TO SUMMIT

5.6

CHEATER STICK EMPLOYED

5.10

CANDY STRIPING

5.12

5.9

5.8

5.8

5.7

5.7

1,300 FEET

Glenn Randall

**Big Rock Candy's Childhood's End** route, a **5.12** difficulty free climb or a **5.10 A0** aid climb. **Each** number indicates the difficulty rating between belay stations (**X**).

ROB MASINTER LEADS THE 5.10 PITCH UP ONE OF BIG ROCK CANDY MOUNTAIN'S WATER GROOVES.

Shortly Rob joined me, collected himself and cast off from our belay to try the next pitch, rated 5.10. He stemmed up one of the symmetric water grooves using single crystals to gain bolts spaced every seven to ten feet. As I followed, my feet smeared across the rock and my hands clawed at fingertip and fingernail sized holds. Wind gusts threatened to pry me loose. It was taking more and more guts to continue upwards. With the climbing just below my limit and no threatening weather, the only thing causing me to contemplate retreat was the unsettling prospect of the lack of protection and our exposed setting hundreds of feet up the cliff.

From the belay at the top of Rob's last lead where we now rested together, I looked up at the next pitch. I saw only four bolts, two in front of my nose and two 150 feet higher at the next belay. The lack of bolts between us and the top of *Childhood's End* implied a maximum fall of 300 feet if I lost my footing just below the upper bolts—a prospect exponentially more daunting than the mere 60-foot fall I'd faced below.

I considered what was before me. No, I wouldn't die if I fell, but surely the injuries would be career-limiting, and who would care if I succeeded? These days my self worth was measured increasingly by rock climbing. Ascending these long, protectionless pitches would mean I had passed *Childhood End's* test. I took the lead.

I climbed at first very carefully, testing each foot's smeared placement, for there were no hand holds at all now. The wind threatened my tenuous friction. As I moved upward, the length of my potential fall increased.

Rob Masinter

THE SOUTH PLATTE RIVER COURSES THROUGH WILDCAT CANYON AT THE
BASE OF BIG ROCK CANDY MOUNTAIN. IN THE FOREGROUND, ROB FRIC-
TIONS UP THE BASE OF THE CANDY-STRIPED SECTION, FORMED BY AGES OF
WATER INCISING THE ROCK. ONLY SMALL DISHES AND EDGES ON WHICH THE
FEET ARE SMEARED MAKE IT POSSIBLE FOR THE CLIMBER TO ASCEND THE
SLAB. FOR ROB, FRICTION CLIMBING IS ESPECIALLY HARD BECAUSE HE CLIMBS
WITH A PROSTHETIC FOOT.

Instead of tightening up and letting thoughts of the consequences impede
my progress, I climbed faster and more fluidly the further I got from
Rob's belay. Each step became less encumbered by concerns about falling
as I was more and more committed to my venture. It became just me and
the rock.

By the end of the pitch I moved with continuous motion, a rare
occurrence for me while rock climbing. On reaching the belay I felt giddy.
I had proven I could climb essentially without protection and found it
liberating. Here, where there was no reason to slow down, I had found a
fluidity of motion on the rock heretofore not experienced except during ski
races.

The rewards of freedom required risk. I was empowered by my ability
to overcome both the physical and psychological challenges of this climb.

THE AUTHOR EXECUTES HIS CONSCIOUS DECISION TO TASTE THE SWEET FREEDOM OFFERED BY THE UPPER THREE NEARLY PROTECTIONLESS PITCHES ON BIG ROCK CANDY MOUNTAIN.

Two more protectionless 5.6 pitches led us to the summit. Rob let me lead both. I couldn't get enough of flexing my risk muscles on this smooth rock. While I hadn't reached any physical limit, I had jumped a psychological barrier, that now cleared, gave me confidence to contemplate still greater challenges.

Breaking out of the reverie of our success on *Childhood's End*, we rappelled 200 feet down the backside of Big Rock Candy Mountain, back to earth, where we grabbed previously stashed mountain bikes and rode a speedy descent back to the car. After driving about five of the 15 miles out of the canyon, we happened on a lone hound dog dragging ass up the road. This dog sulked over to the car and whimpered.

Rob looked at me and said with a sheepish grin, "I bet this is the 'wolf' from last night." One look at the dog revealed the hyperbole of our fears. This wolf-sized animal now looked more like dehydrated mountain lion bait.

We loaded the wolf-turned-hound dog into the back seat and gave it water and our last peanut butter and jelly sandwich. Five miles into an altruistic delivery mission to the Colorado Springs dog pound, we met a Jeep coming towards us.

"Did you guys see a brown hound dog?" The driver asked.

I saw a spark of recognition on his face as he looked in our back seat.

"I've been looking for that dog since last night. It's my roommate's six-month old puppy."

**THE DESCENT.**

**DAVE SULESKI RUNS *QUARTZITE FALLS* ON ARIZONA'S SALT RIVER IN 1994,
ONE YEAR AFTER DYNAMITE WAS USED TO BREAK DOWN THE ROCK BARRIER
HERE THAT PREVIOUSLY MADE *QUARTZITE FALLS* AN UNRUNNABLE CLASS 6
WATERFALL.**

# Arizona's Salt River

*Comes a time when you're driftin'*
—Neil Young

## STARTING OUT WITH A BLAST

I grew up in New York and Vermont where my only whitewater action was either of the frozen sort on the ski slopes or tubing a mile or so down to the local swimming hole. I had no experience in a kayak.

I had always reasoned that if I was knocked unconscious from a fall while rock climbing, I could continue breathing 'till I came to. Suffering such an event kayaking would result in permanent unconsciousness.

My first river trip in a canoe, and two raft trips a year earlier, had opened my mind to whitewater's peculiar character. I could see that kayaking seemed similar to skiing—moving down hill, around rocks and through chutes—only the medium was in motion.

It was in the context of a widely-reported accident and its aftermath that I started to change my adrenaline sport of choice from rock climbing to whitewater kayaking.

The accident occurred in May 1993, two days after I returned from my first whitewater kayak trip on Arizona's Salt River. An article in the *Phoenix Sun* described a harrowing episode wherein two rafters died on the Salt River's *Quartzite Falls*. The rafters chose to run a waterfall that was invariably portaged by everyone. The three men in the party clung for minutes to their bucking raft as it was recirculated in and out of the pounding vertical curtain of water at the base of the falls. They tried to swim for safety. One made it to an island, another was swept downstream to his death and the third was pulled back into the falls where he drowned.

This story hit home immediately. For I realized my friend, Dave Suleski, and I were likely the last to have seen this group. As it turned out our involvement with these falls was not over. Dave and I, just one year later would be the first party to expose an act of eco-terrorism at *Quartzite Falls*, an act that was indirectly related to the rafter's deaths and one that would raise environmental, regulatory and ethical issues.

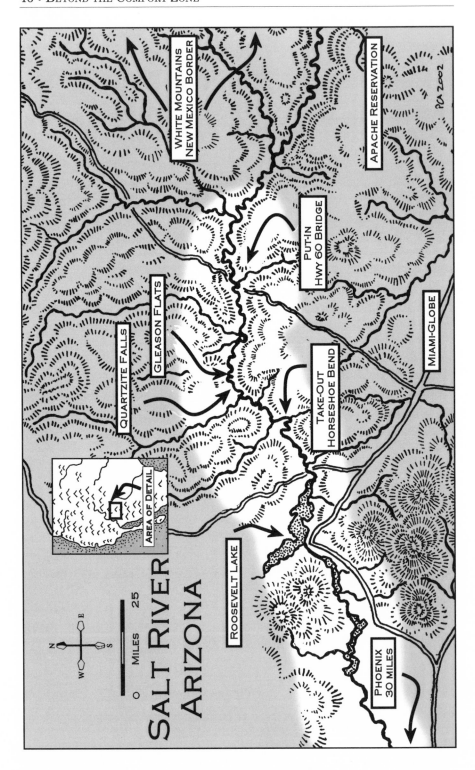

PCA 2002

WHITE MOUNTAINS
NEW MEXICO BORDER

APACHE RESERVATION

PUT-IN
HWY 60 BRIDGE

MIAMI-GLOBE

QUARTZITE FALLS

GLEASON FLATS

TAKE-OUT
HORSESHOE BEND

AREA OF DETAIL

ROOSEVELT LAKE

SALT RIVER
ARIZONA

N
W    E
S

0    MILES    25

PHOENIX
30 MILES

Arizona had received record precipitation that previous winter. The Salt River, which drains the 9,000 to 10,000-foot peaks of the White Mountains on the border of New Mexico and Arizona, normally peaks in early spring with a 10,000 cubic feet per second[1] flow (half that found in the Colorado River through Grand Canyon during average summer flows). That winter, combinations of heavy snows followed by torrential downpours caused the Salt River to rise to a recent record of 126,000 cubic feet per second, scouring the canyon walls and vibrating pilings on the state highway bridge.

Dave, who lived near the river in Miami-Globe, Arizona, monitored the flow all winter and started paddling the river in his whitewater kayak when it receded to safe levels. Kayaking was his new passion, but at his level of experience, he needed a partner because he still occasionally missed his roll and swam—an activity that requires rescue on serious whitewater rivers.

"Bruce, the Salt is running at a perfect level," he entreated. I was living in Phoenix at the time. Dave had been a major instigator of fun and extreme activities in my recreational life that year. Most recently, I joined him (albeit in a canoe) on a one-day trip down a section of the Gila River, a few hundred miles south. I found the Gila's scenery stunning and the paddling physically challenging. But, I knew from friends, guidebooks and magazines that bigger, more challenging rivers awaited.

Now, he was proposing another adventure and a chance to try something new. I remembered a kayaker in Colorado compare rafting and kayaking by saying, "Get off the bus and into a sports car." Driving a sports car implied maneuverability at the edge of control, an experience I generally sought.

Dave was itching to continue on the final, roadless 42 miles of the Salt River canyon that he had yet to kayak. Due to his strong canoeing background from his youth in Wisconsin, he was undaunted by whitewater kayaking.

"The water level is coming down. It'll only last a few more weeks. We should run the whole canyon," Dave said, conscious of the ephemeral nature of desert river flows.

I thought for a moment. I was in the thick of training for an attempt on El Capitan's *Nose* route, and was reluctant to be distracted. Soon I suspected I'd feel satisfied with the diversity of climbs I had done and

---

1. Cubic feet per second (cfs) is the unit of measure of water volume passing by the shore each second. Boaters generally refer to this measure as the "flow." Each river has a unique relationship between flow and difficulty. Generally, the higher the flow, the more difficult and certainly the more committing one's trip will be. Our timing on the Salt was intended to make our passage easier.

places climbing had taken me. Most of my recent climbing had been of the solo sort. So, the prospect of group adventures in river canyons helped push me towards accepting Dave's offer. My last thought was of my concern about drowning while kayaking. This had eased because climbing had expanded my comfort zone, making the risks of whitewater kayaking somehow more acceptable.

I relented, "What is the deal? How do you do it? I don't even have a kayak."

"Three days, two nights to do the 52 miles. It's all Class 3 and 4 rapids.[2] There is only one Class 6, *Quartzite Falls*, and the guidebook says you can portage around it. We can do it." He said.

I didn't know Class 3 from 4, but I did know Class 6 was unrunnable. I had never seen an unrunnable rapid before, except for Niagra Falls. My thoughts shifted into action after work when I headed over to the local REI and looked at their "for sale" board and saw a Perception Dancer whitewater kayak for sale. Four hundred dollars later I was outfitted. That Thursday, I took off from work and headed to the mountains to meet Dave.

First things first, I would have to learn the roll. Dave also needed practice on his. Using a book for guidance, we took our boats down to Roosevelt Lake at the bottom of the Upper Salt River Canyon. There we tried to teach each other the Eskimo roll. Dave could right himself after a deliberate capsize about 50% of the time. Out of 20 tries, I succeeded once. I was confused trying to translate written instructions into physical action while water trickled in my nose and I blindly thrashed about upside down. I knew I couldn't kayak this river without a roll, but the allure of the river and the small window of time to catch a good water flow level compelled me to consider the risk regardless of my inability to roll.

As we continued to practice, two kayakers paddled down the river and pulled ashore before us. They looked spent. It took them five days to do what we planned to do in three. Right then Dave decided to shorten our trip by 15 miles.

"Do you guys have any food we can have?" They asked.

"Trade you some oranges for rolling lessons," Dave responded.

---

2. River difficulty is described, much like rock climbing grades, from a low number (easier) to a higher number (harder). Class 1 is flat water. Class 6 is considered unrunnable. The difference between Class 3 and 4 is that Class 4 requires maneuvering to avoid rocks and holes. Class 5 is defined as must-make maneuvering to avoid possibly fatal obstacles. Class 6 indicates that the obstacles are unavoidable and fatal.

Dave's success rate rose to about 90% and mine to 50%. I rode along in the car toward the put-in, still concerned. Swimming free of your kayak was the equivalent to falling rock climbing. Unlike rock climbing, a "fall" kayaking would not be arrested by a rope. A swim would put me at the mercy of the river.

While running our shuttle on a back road to the river, we bumped into the local search and rescue team.

"Were you on the river?" They asked.

"No, but we will be tomorrow," Dave answered.

"We are here to do a body recovery. There was an accident. A rafter drowned somewhere upstream. If you see the body, tie it off to a tree or bush or rock and mark on your map where it is," they instructed. This accident was different than the one at *Quartzite Falls*, which had yet to occur.

I sat in shocked silence. First an experienced team had taken five days to do what was supposed to take three, I didn't have a reliable roll and now there was a dead body on the river.

"Dave, this sounds pretty hard core," I remarked.

I was reminded of my first trip to ski the extreme couloirs of Colorado's Pikes Peak. From the parking lot at the base, I saw a telemark skier drop off of the final cliff of the famed *W Couloir* only to ricochet off of the left wall and break his femur. John, my skiing pal, looked at me and said, "We *have* to ski that." We shared a desire to test ourselves where others had failed. Here on the Salt, I wasn't deterred by the plight of someone who had also suffered the consequences inherent in extreme sports (sporting activities where a screw up means death or debilitating injury). What didn't settle in my head was that the consequences of an accident on whitewater tended to be fatal compared to merely acute injuries resulting from skiing and climbing accidents.

In the few hours before we reached the put-in, I searched the how-to kayak book for enough information on river technique to let me survive our intended outing. During our roll practice I realized the spray skirt for my boat leaked. I sewed a new elastic on with dental floss.

The next morning Dave and I stuffed our boats with the bare minimum of gear

**PIKES PEAK'S W COULOIRS.**

and food for two nights. I jammed my Teva sandals in last, expecting to use them if I had to portage. I looked around before getting into my boat and considered my upcoming adventure. We were to paddle 37 miles, starting from country sufficiently high and wet enough to support pine trees, through innumerable bends and canyons and down 100 separate rapids, ending in the Sonoran Desert. Our reality was that after the first ten miles, our only escape would be by walking 20 miles through mountainous desert country adorned by a deceptively dense "forest" of cactus. This level of commitment made almost all of my rock climbing and mountaineering adventures pale by comparison. Rock climbing seemed suddenly so predictable. With kayaking the challenge changed constantly and remained in my face.

When I slid into the river above the first rapid, I immediately noticed a sluggishness in my boat that had not been there during our roll practice the day before. The weight of my overnight gear added a new layer of challenge to an already daunting task.

We scouted the first rapid from shore. It plowed directly into a rock wall. Dave went first, and on seeing him still upright, clear of the wall and headed downstream, I willingly paddled after him.

As I entered the current, I felt it grab me. The book hadn't described the acceleration of the current or the feeling of being at the mercy of the river. I felt out of control. Desperate paddle flailings kept me upright. I looked back with exhilaration, flushed with excitement at having unwittingly found something that rushed me immediately toward the edge of my ability. Soon I would learn, this gold-plating on the experience was deceptive in its seeming forgiveness.

As we floated along, flush with success and expectation, Dave looked over and said, "You know, there is no one else I would rather be doing this with." The feeling was mutual. Through serendipitously meeting Dave some years before, the inspirational river/canyon setting and my innate reaction to the challenge, I was nearly hooked on kayaking. I took my first swim on the next rapid, but easily collected my boat and gear in a pool at its base. I had expected to swim and took my first dousing in stride.

On the next rapid, aptly called *Overboard,* my greatest fear of kayaking was realized. As we neared the rapid, whitewater crashed over rocks below and the rapid disappeared around a curve below. I felt a small pang of fear and tensed up, uncertain of how to tackle this rapid. This time I could see that a swim here would have far greater consequences than the one I had just taken.

I tried desperately to maneuver to shore for I couldn't read the water to discern a safe line. As my bow scraped the shore, the current grabbed my stern and dragged me backwards into the accelerating tongue of water leading to the rapid.

With slaps to my back, the first series of waves engulfed my boat. I hit a partially submerged rock and spun around moments before a second rock and hole below it caught my boat sideways. I flipped upstream. Rolling up never crossed my mind. I was swept downstream, head down. I instinctively dropped my paddle and prepared to release the spray skirt that sealed me and my overnight gear in the boat.

As I bent forward to reach the release loop, my face smashed into a rock. My head snapped backwards and my torso slammed on my kayak's rear deck. I saw stars and pain shot through my face, head and neck.

**THE AUTHOR'S WORST NIGHTMARE WAS REALIZED ON THE THIRD RAPID ON HIS FIRST WHITEWATER KAYAK TRIP ON ARIZONA'S SALT RIVER.**

I threw my hands up around my face to protect myself as I banged into more rocks with my helmet and shoulders. Desperate for a breath, I reached forward for the release loop despite a gripping fear of hitting my face again. This time, I reached the skirt and squirmed out of my kayak, clawing for the surface.

As I tumbled through the final rocks and waves of the rapid, straining desperately for an occasional breath, my face slammed into my runaway kayak numerous times as my kayak was slowed by surface froth and I was carried on by faster, deeper water. I gasped air when I could and felt my lungs convulse for air when I was held down. Just when I started to fear I was going to drown, the rapid relented and I floated into a pool.

Nearly exhausted from oxygen deprivation, I dog-paddled shoreward. Dave chased down my boat. Compounding my commitment that day, I saw my sandals floating away as I dragged myself onto the rocks. I realized then that kayaking exacted a much higher price for a mistake than climbing ever had. My indulgence in running a river above my abilities had not only nearly knocked me out and drowned me, but now any option I had for hiking out had just floated downstream.

What scared and thrilled me about rock climbing were heights, getting just to the edge of falling, and the overall physical challenge. However, rock climbing's dangers are generally controllable and self-determined as *I* could decide just how high I would go and *if* I was going to make that one marginal move risking a fall. Here, on the third rapid of the river, I had found myself nearly drowning with little chance to do anything about my plight. In my naivete, what had happened was like falling from the third handhold of a 10-pitch climb and getting scrapes and a twisted ankle. Continuing kayaking would force me to take risks comparable to unroped rock climbing or mountaineering in the "death zone" above about 20,000 feet altitude. I had only dabbled with unroped climbing. I wasn't yet at a stage in my life where the thrill I received from adrenaline sports had to be increased by interjecting knowledge that I had cheated the biggest consequence, death, during my fleeting thrill ride.

I put my trauma in a different compartment and got back in my shoeless boat. What kept me going might have been the fact that I enjoyed the challenge of conquering the personal subordination required by the river. Or, maybe my motivation to continue was the fact that I wasn't physically blocked from continuing, unlike a too-difficult rock move, but only blocked by rapids that hadn't killed me yet, and, given their moderate difficultly, were probably not likely to kill me.

I swam scores of times that day. Yet I found the excitement of kayaking was what I had been searching for. This new sport held me at the edge and occasionally beyond my comfort zone all day. That night we camped on a deserted beach. I watched in awe as the relentless current flowed beside the first saguaro cacti of the canyon. I likened kayaking the river to riding the back of a serpent.

Despite being in the best physical shape of my life—due to the six-month training regime I had been under for my upcoming attempt on El Capitan in Yosemite—I woke up sore, a sure testament to the punishment I had taken the day before. As we prepared to put back on the river, we watched a lone kayaker effortlessly float and spin, down rapids that made me tense just looking at them. In two daylight hours, this kayaker had descended the same 11 miles that had taken us most of the previous day. I could have been demoralized by the gulf of ability, but I found myself simply inspired to attain the same level of comfort.

As we started down the river that morning, I was tense, having suffered so much the day before. It felt as if *Quartzite Falls* was always just around the next corner. After nearly every rapid, we consulted Dave's mile-by-mile guide. *Quartzite Falls* was described as a two-tiered cascade totaling 12 feet that poured between 500-foot tall, nearly bulletproof quartzite rock cliffs. We had heard the river-level portage entailed 5.2 difficulty rock climbing, a level that could be challenging when attempted while carrying loaded kayaks.

A common belief was that the consequences of running this waterfall were fatal. Upstream and downstream currents converged at the base of the falls, pinning a victim underwater. If I kept up my record of a swim at nearly every rapid, a swim before *Quartzite* might be my last.

As we kayaked along, I couldn't pinpoint what had changed for me, but I found my balance and had not flipped recently in any rapids. However, on one unnamed rapid, Dave capsized and swam free of his boat and paddle. He became pinned against a rock wall near the base of the rapid. As I passed him, desperately stabbing the water with my paddle to avoid capsizing myself, I saw him rock climb straight out of the water. His boat continued on, forcing me to give chase as he had to mine so many times before. Class 4 *Black Rock* rapid loomed a hundred yards ahead, providing ample incentive for my first boat rescue.

I chased his boat downstream and, just as I started to nudge it towards shore, I flipped. Dave, standing fifty yards upstream, was powerless to help. My normal modus operandi post capsize was to swim, which likely would likely send me swimming through *Black Rock* rapid. And, if I was unable to corral mine and Dave's boats, a shoeless, cactus-rich, scorching desert hike of epic proportions loomed for our team. Swimming downstream after our boats was out of the question because *Quartzite Falls* was next. This was a must-make situation.

I tried one roll and failed. My lungs convulsed and screamed for air. I tried another roll and failed. Instinct told me to bail and save myself from drowning, but consequences flashed through my brain. I had to make one final effort or regret for miles and days that I didn't try one last time.

Concentrating on technique, I reached for the surface with my paddle, setting up for the roll. I swept my paddle across the surface, did a hip snap and sure enough, my head rocketed above water so fast that I teetered, nearly toppling over the other side. Hyperventilating from oxygen deprivation, I stabilized, reached Dave's boat and drove it to shore where I slumped over my deck and counted our blessings. He jumped in upstream and swam an angled path across the current.

Shortly before *Quartzite Falls* was a two-mile-long flat section of river called Gleason Flats, where the canyon walls receded to the distance. There we met an upstream wind. As we paddled into the wind, we reveled in the space and solitude of the river and its canyon. To get to where we were by vehicle or foot would have taken hours of rugged four wheeling or hiking. We were seated comfortably in our kayaks, spinning in the current, savoring awesome scenery.

Ahead, a raft filled with three men struggled downstream against the wind. The men were older than us, perhaps in their early forties, and by the looks of their equipment, seasoned river rats.

"Beautiful day, eh?" I said by way of greeting.

The looked down at us from their raft perch and one said, "It would be nicer if there weren't so many new people using the river."

I was taken aback. I was a newcomer to the river.

"We've been running this river for 10 years now. It is getting too popular," one of them said.

I realized quickly that they wanted to pull the door shut behind them, preserving their self-actualizing wilderness experience at the expense of others.

**GLEASON FLATS.**

"Hope you guys have a nice day," I said and paddled ahead.

Through my climbing experience I understood the desire of some early ascensionists to forsake the fame of reporting their first ascents for maintenance of the untrammeled nature of their route and its location. For to publish a guide to an area was to invite crowds and inevitable regulation. But, here on the Salt River, our use of the river was unencumbered, and the guide we used was published years before. I wasn't going to subordinate my rights just because exercising them rankled someone else.

The river walls narrowed as we left the disquieting waters of Gleason Flats. My geology training told me the rising cliffs were quartzite rock, our first clue we were nearing *Quartzite Falls*. The current picked up pace.

Cliffs rose hundreds of feet straight up. We rounded a corner, and there in the distance the river disappeared over a misty horizon line. *Quartzite Falls* loomed.

We nervously stopped at the first landing spot we could find. I joined Dave at a vantage point high above the falls. We looked obliquely down on the twin, nearly linear, white lines across the river. The second fall dumped into a pool that was bounded by rock walls. The pool's outlet led to a Class 4 rapid named *Corkscrew*.

We jabbered on about what we saw. The falls met every expectation that had been built. In my estimation, they were unrunnable.

The portage around the falls was tedious, but easier than expected. We put our boats into the river in the pool below the falls. Just ten feet away was the awesome power of the second fall. I could see the current on the surface streaming back upstream to meet the curtain of water. It was deadly beautiful.

As we scouted at river level, I could see rock climbing type bolts in the far walls among a jumble of car- and truck-sized boulders.

**QUARTZITE FALLS BEFORE MODIFICATION.**

"I think that is where the commercial trips line their rafts through," Dave said.

"The clients walk along the shore?" I asked.

"Yep, I think it takes three hours or so, apparently adding a day to a commercial trip down the river," Dave said. The significance of this dialog would not dawn on me until a year later, when a second tragedy at *Quartzite Falls* occurred.

After *Quartzite* I steeled myself for an inevitable swim in *Corkscrew* rapid. The river plunged steeply and turned sharply left where a six-foot-tall wave broke over my head. I accepted the consequences of poor technique and inexperience. Dave fished me out.

On rapids where the water was less turbulent I learned to stay upright and avoid the roll altogether. By the end of the day, Dave and I grew comfortable enough to take a look around for the dead body of the raft guide from the first accident. We never saw it. By the end of the trip to Horseshoe Bend I was relaxed in my new setting.

---

Two days later, through the *Phoenix Sun* article, I learned the fate of the Gleason Flats rafters. The three seasoned rafters chose to run *Quartzite Falls* that afternoon just after we received a dose of their philosophy. Two of them paid the ultimate price.

The story should have become a lesson to me of the failure of ability to tame a river, but that lesson would not be driven home for five years. It did show me the ineffectiveness of a seniority-derived presumption of a preferred right and the coincident need to prove ability to others. While rock climbing I had seen similar attitudes backfire and manifest themselves in extreme behaviors, but never in death. Rivers were unforgiving to even the experienced.

The next year I had all but given up rock climbing for kayaking and, despite moving to Denver, never forgot the Salt River. That spring we caught the first runoff in the Rocky Mountains—back in Arizona. The new kayakers accompanying us had heard our story all too many times and feared *Quartzite Falls* as we had on our first descent.

After two days on the river, we dutifully stopped above the falls and crept downstream to look. The falls were gone. The parallel horizon lines were gone. There was no mist, no impediment to river travellers. The bullet-hard quartzite was broken. The river ran through the cliff faces in a nearly-smooth tongue. What had been Class 6 was now Class 3. We were shocked. On the far shore I saw traces of red on the rock. Dave thought it looked like dynamite residue.

Upon returning to the put-in to retrieve our car, we stopped into the trading post where we had purchased the unlimited-use permits issued by the San Carlos Apache. "Did you know *Quartzite Falls* is gone?" We asked. They thought we were joking.

A flurry of legal, administrative and environmental activity resulted. The perpetrators who blasted the falls were caught, tried and sentenced. They claimed they eliminated the twin death-falls to protect others from the fate of the Gleason Flats raft crew.

The court of public opinion weighed in on the subject through stories in national publications and regional papers. Some observers suggested that, because those who blasted the falls were raft guides (whose business would be more efficient if the bottleneck portage at *Quartzite Falls* was eliminated), that there may have been an economic component to their motivations.

I believe that if you choose to descend a river, you do it at your own risk. Removing the scary and deadly crux on the Salt River did nothing to stop the erosion of personal accountability pervading parts of our society.

This act of misguided altruism and environmental and economic terrorism put the Salt River into the national recreational limelight with articles in magazines with national distribution, such as Outside. The resulting publicity on this desert river, now emasculated, drove up demand. The forest service imposed a permit system the next year, erecting a high hurdle before new and old users alike.

The private rafters who died on *Quartzite Falls* did not become martyrs, but, ironically, catalysts for the exact opposite of the change they professed to want.

BRAD SCHILDT, THE AUTHOR, DAVE SULESKI AND RICK WINTERS AT HORSE-SHOE BEND ON THE SALT RIVER, APRIL 1994. IT WAS DURING THIS TRIP THAT THEY FOUND *QUARTZITE FALLS* BLOWN UP.

John Hill

FROM THE EDGE OF HALF DOME'S 5,000-FOOT DROP, THE AUTHOR CONTEM-
PLATES HIS RECENT FAILURE ON EL CAPITAN'S *NOSE* ROUTE. IT WOULD TAKE
A SECOND TRY TO SUCCEED. THE PROFILE OF THE *NOSE* IS VISIBLE, CURVING
UPWARD 3,000 FEET FROM THE VALLEY FLOOR IN THE MIDDLE DISTANCE.

# Yosemite's El Capitan

*Freedom's just another word for nothing left to lose*
*ME AND BOBBY MCGEE* —Kris Kristofferson

## NIHILISM ON THE *BIG STONE*

THROUGHOUT MY 20S, MY DESIRE TO PROGRESS TOWARDS GRANDER ROCK CLIMBS OUTPACED MY ABILITY. BUT, AS WITH OTHER CHALLENGES, I PERSISTED TILL I SUCCEEDED. BRIDGING MY 27TH TO 29TH YEARS, THIS STORY CAPS MY ROCK CLIMBING CAREER.

El Capitan's *Nose* is the epitome of a "big-wall" route. It requires tenacity, persistence and teamwork to climb its 3,000 vertical feet. Devious tactics and complex logistics distinguish it as it shifts from one crack system to another. It rears to an intimidating 30-foot overhang on its final pitch.

The *Nose* has become a proving ground for big-wall aspirants and a finishing ground for experienced big-wall climbers who come from all over the world to Yosemite to test themselves against its undisputed standard.

JOHN HILL, ONE OF THE AUTHOR'S CLIMBING PARTNERS, CONSIDERS THE *BIG STONE* IN JUNE 1991. FROM BASE TO SUMMIT, EL CAPITAN'S FACE MEASURES 2,898 FEET. THE *NOSE* FOLLOWS THE SHADOW LINE UP THE CENTER OF THE CLIFF. BECAUSE THE CLIMBING ROUTE FOLLOWS DISCONTINUOUS CRACKS WHICH FORCE IT TO MEANDER AND, AT SOME POINTS, DESCEND, MOST CALL IT AN EVEN 3,000-FOOT CLIMB.

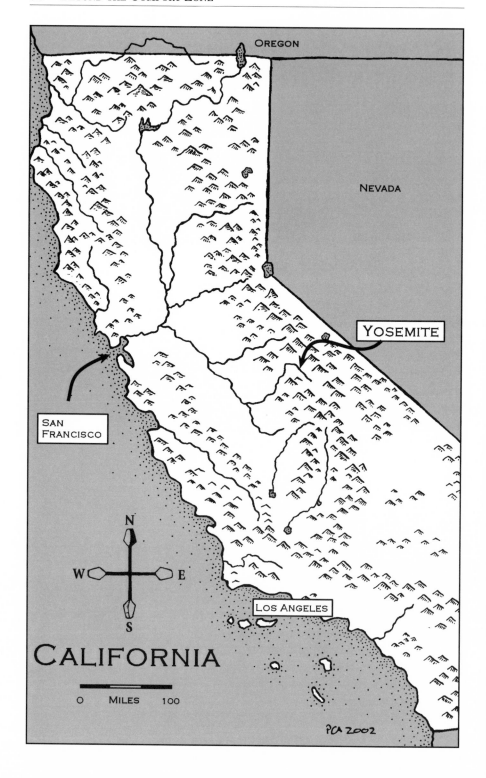

It ascends the longest uninterrupted vertical expanse of granite in the lower 48 states. First climbed in 1958, over 45 days, today's teams take three to six days, bivouacking on natural ledges. The fastest climbers have ascended the route in less than four hours. I simply aspired to four or five days.

Our idea to climb the *Nose* arose one fall evening in 1990, after a climbing session in Boulder Canyon, Colorado. Brad Schildt, John Hill and I, all college classmates, had recently finished graduate school and had energy and resources to burn. We schemed about the "next greater" rock climb, mountaineering trip or ski descent. We thrived on accomplishing the athletic test pieces that were held in high regard by our peers and mentors. Outside of work I found my identity defined and enhanced by my rock climbing progress; therefore an attempt on an El Capitan route seemed a necessary step in my personal growth. Success, I thought, would bolster my self-esteem.

THE AUTHOR, JOHN HILL AND BRAD SCHILDT ON TOP OF *THE NAKED EDGE*, III 5.11 IN ELDORADO CANYON, COLORADO IN 1990. IT WAS AFTER CLIMBS SUCH AS THIS AND *THE CASUAL ROUTE* ON LONGS PEAK'S *DIAMOND* THAT MADE A CLIMB OF EL CAPITAN PLAUSIBLE.

We bought the guidebook, researched the route and soon committed ourselves. Our plans were regularly described to friends, unwittingly building expectations to the extent that I intended to measure our success only by our complete ascent of the *Nose*. The challenge of climbing such a face was so romantic that I invested all of my excess energy in it—to the detriment of personal relationships.

I dreamt of leaving a mark for my descendants and immediate family, much like my great-uncle who became the youngest Master of a San Francisco-based, square-rigged cargo ship at the age of 18 and could climb hand-over-hand to the first yardarm; or like a high school friend who told of his father swimming some 20 miles across Lake Champlain in Vermont as a young man. These feats had seemed unattainable to me, but now, with rock climbing, I saw my chance to establish a reputation.

There existed deeper motivations as well. Influencing my behavior at the time was my dysfunctional relationship with my father. As with many other youths who push themselves beyond reasonable measures of risk or into rebellious behavior, I too found myself seeking his attention and approval. Fortunately my expression came on mountains and rivers, not bars and streets. My attention-seeking behavior netted me success on many difficult climbs as I tried to work out my angst.

Our attempt on El Capitan was set for June 1991. All winter, Brad, John and I teamed up for indoor training sessions at local rock gyms. I lifted weights during lunch, ran and soon considered myself at a new height of physical conditioning. Eventually, spring days lengthened and our horizons expanded, allowing weekday training sessions at Eldorado Canyon south of Boulder, North Table Mountain, Clear Creek Canyon near Golden, and Morrison.

On weekends we traveled to train on longer and more difficult rock where we tried to teach ourselves to aid climb, a climbing technique that we knew would get us up sections of the *Nose* that were beyond our free-climbing abilities.

Late in May, we packed overnight gear and even a few rocks in our newly-purchased haul bag to simulate real big-wall conditions, but the bag only weighed 50 lbs., less than half what it would on the *Nose*. Our intent was to spend the night on the side of a local cliff. Poor execution and lack of sleeping ledges on our training route foiled the plan. Our ambition blinded us to the reality that our first real practice climb would be in Yosemite.

Our attempt of the *Nose* was the talk of parties. We were coached and cautioned from the sofas of Boulder and Denver. I basked in the attention and my conjecture of future adulation. Shallow, vain responses, but true nonetheless. I had doubts, having never tried a climb of the *Nose's* magnitude, but being within the comfortable confines of my daily life in Denver, I easily masked them or rationalized them away, all the while marching inevitably towards the actual climb.

SOCIAL OBLIGATIONS, WEATHER, LOGISTICS AND BUSINESS RESPONSIBILITIES CONSPIRED TO MAKE OUR TRAINING DIFFICULT. ABOVE, A TYPICAL "INDOOR TRAINING SESSION."

Brad identified our roles on each pitch of the climb and marked our map accordingly. He could lead 5.10 consistently, John would lead routes as difficult as 5.8, and I would lead on routes as difficult as 5.9. We rationalized that we would aid climb the sections beyond our ability and breeze up those pitches rated at or below our free-climbing ability.[1] Our training, while intended to be rigorous, was constrained regularly by social obligations and late season snow and rain in Colorado's front range.

June came, we flew to San Francisco, our game faces on and as ready as we thought we could be. We rented a Chrysler Fifth Avenue full-sized luxury sedan, big enough for our gear and our egos. We intended to roll into Yosemite and attempt, without taking any prerequisites, the biggest wall it had to offer. Stable and hot weather was forecast—good climbing weather—in contrast to the cool Colorado rain in which we had trained.

The *Nose* is divided into four sections (see map on next page). Our plan called for us to ascend the first four pitches in one day, which would lead us to the four-foot wide and 150-foot long Sickle Ledge. Next, we would complete two sequential pendulums, which would move us across the cliff to the 400-foot long hand-sized crack called the "Stovelegs" (so named because first ascensionist Warren Harding used legs from a junk stove as pitons here). This crack led to El Cap Towers, where we intended to bivouac. After resting there on bunk bed-sized ledges 1,500 feet up, we would continue by tackling the flake and pendulum section—defined by Texas Flake, Boot Flake and the King Swing—that led to Camp Four. Finally, the love-seat sized sloping ledges of Camp Four would be the stage from where we would attack the sweeping and overhanging cracks leading through the Great Roof, Camps Five and Six and on to the summit. Our goal was to do each section in ten to twelve hours and we had planned supplies accordingly.

Our gear included a standard ensemble or "rack" of camming devices, carabiners and chocks, three ropes and assorted gear for aid climbing. In addition, we brought along our "stickus," or cheater stick, a reaching device that we considered a magic wand. We used it to reach up and clip pitons, bolt hangers or fixed protection so that the difficulties directly above us could be easily climbed by hand-over-hand ascent of the webbing that dangled from the top of the stick. We had adopted a "success over style" philosophy, bred from our acknowledged lack of skills, and possibly unconsciously from our over-spoken expectation of success.

Logistics on the *Nose* are complex. Three main tasks must be accomplished on each 100-foot pitch: lead, ascend/clean and raise the haul bag. We would alternate roles on each pitch. Brad would lead while I

---

1. The *Nose* route has a rating of 5.11, 80% of which is rated 5.9 or harder.

Brad Schildt

**BRAD SCHILDT CARRIES A TYPICAL AID RACK ON THE 50TH ASCENT OF STANDING ROCK IN CANYONLANDS.**

belayed him from below. As soon as he reached the next belay station, John would fix two mechanical devices on the rope and "jümar", or ascend, while cleaning, or removing, the gear Brad placed. I would then free the "pig," or haul bag, from its tether at the lower belay so that Brad could raise it to his position. Finally, I would then ascend the remaining fixed rope and join them at the upper station.

On easier ground we expected to spend 1.5 hours per pitch. When the going got tough, our leader would be forced to carry aid gear on his rack (up to 20 lbs. extra weight). Compound this added weight with tricky logistics on some pitches—like penduluming from one crack to another—and each aid pitch could take three hours. We naively hoped to be able to keep the longest pitch down to two hours.

We approached the wall seemingly prepared for its challenges. But, that day we learned lesson after lesson. The haul bag nearly fell to the ground as the knot on one of our pieces of webbing slipped open. On each pitch that was not vertical, the haul bag tumbled sideways when released, threatening to split open or rupture its cargo of precious water bottles. Leading required adroit problem-solving skills and devious tactics never demanded by our training climbs. All the while we were forced to regularly trust ancient-looking bolts and pitons, a practice rarely done deliberately in my climbing history.

As early as the second belay, the nearly-overwhelming nature of the route hit home. There, despite our best intentions, we faced a jumble of carabiners, chocks, camming devices, webbing, three bodies, fear, uncertainty, discomfort and intensity. Three men and the inanimate haul bag hung from one new bolt, two rusty pitons and one of our camming devices. There was no ledge here, just smooth granite plunging straight to

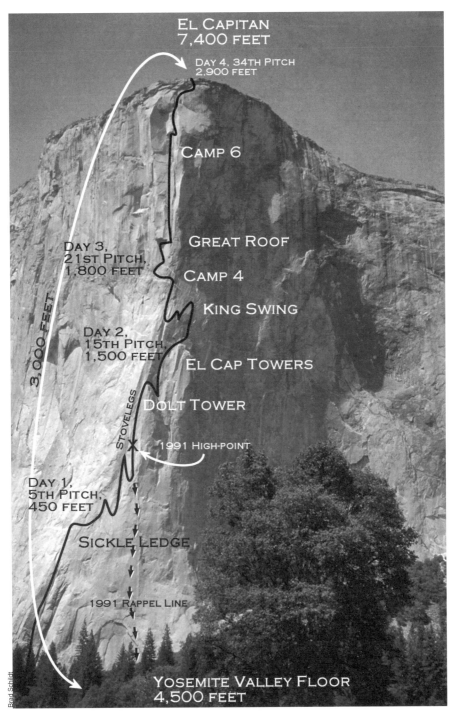

EL CAPITAN'S *NOSE* ROUTE, ITS SIGNIFICANT FEATURES AND THE AUTHOR'S
1991 AND 1993 SCHEDULES.

the ground. Untangling and sorting ropes and gear was complicated by the fact that every carabiner held at least one of us. We bumped, prodded and addled each other as we hung from our short tethers. Furthermore, each action possessed a sense of urgency as our supplies were limited. We felt constant pressure to perform so as to not jeopardize the group's objective. From this mess, the process began again—only 32 more pitches to the top.

While we climbed the first four pitches to Sickle Ledge, Brad kept a careful eye on our progress and noted that we were substantially slower than he expected. He climbed at or above the level he expected to, but realized that even his pace was too slow for the first four pitches, which, in comparison to the rest of the *Nose,* were logistically straightforward.

Despite being physically stronger than both Brad and me, John was increasingly uncomfortable with the exposure and the logistics of this climb. He was slowed to a pace below his physical ability.

We finally reached Sickle Ledge, 450 feet up, by 3pm, dehydrated and disoriented. With the haul bag under tension all day, we could not access our food or water, so we had gone without. The air was about 90 degrees Fahrenheit and the wind blew a steady 10 to 20 mph. These conditions conspired to sap our energy and made it difficult to communicate.

AID CLIMBING AT THE END OF THE FOURTH PITCH, THE AUTHOR REACHES RIGHT TO CLIP A PITON PLACED BY A PREVIOUS PARTY USING THE CUSTOM-MADE CHEATER STICK. OFF IMAGE RIGHT IS SICKLE LEDGE. THE LEAD ROPE ZIG ZAGS AT LEFT. THE HAUL ROPE IS TRAILED AT CENTER.

THE GREAT ROOF AND OVERHANG-ING SUMMIT PITCHES ARE VISIBLE TOP RIGHT.

Below spanned a featureless granite sheet. The one hundred-foot-tall pines of the valley floor now seemed in another world. Sickle Ledge's narrowness kept me so close to the upper wall that when I looked up, its features blended into a vertical mirage.

I felt a growing sense of under preparedness. Having never been staged below such an immense climb, I could not translate my feelings into words or actions. There was nothing in the frustration and slowness of the first day's progress that dissuaded me from following through on my commitment to attempt this climb. As usual, none of us openly discussed our fears—a common malady affecting climbers that occasionally results in over extension of one party.

Gear now secured on sickle ledge, we rappelled and camped at the base of the cliff—hoping for a better night's sleep there than on the airy, narrow Sickle Ledge. Sleep, when it came, was fitful and filled with foreboding, for now it wasn't someone's story or a guide book telling me what to expect, I was experiencing El Capitan first hand. I had committed myself to an unknown logistical, physical and mental exercise. I wasn't on a sofa in Denver anymore.

Recommencing our ascent, we awoke at 3:30am and ascended our ropes that we had left in place the day before. I went first and reached Sickle Ledge by 5am. The jümar ascent was long and strenuous and was completed just as the first light of day brightened the sky to the east over Half Dome.

I felt cold, tense and nearly overwhelmed by the wall looming overhead. While waiting for John and Brad to finish the morning's jümar, I hunkered down, shaking, partly because of the chilly air and partly because I was just plain afraid. My stomach registered hollow. I had consciously chosen to do this climb, wanted badly to follow through on the opportunity I'd created and the vain expectations I had set. I was willing to persevere despite my fear. I was driven to capitalize.

We set ourselves to task. The first pitch above Sickle Ledge was marked as mine—under our assumption that I would lead it quickly without having to resort to aid climbing. However, once climbing, I found my arms so fatigued that I succumbed to aid. A layer of confidence peeled away.

**JUMARING THE FIRST OF THREE ROPES AT THE PREDAWN START OF THE 1991 ATTEMPT.**

Brad Schildt

AT THE HIGH-POINT OF HIS **1991** AT-
TEMPT, THE AUTHOR HANGS FROM A BOLT
AND A CAMMING DEVICE IN THE STOVE-
LEGS CRACK. ASSEMBLED ARE TWO
ROPES, THE LEADER'S RACK, ONE BOXER'S
PUNCHING-BAG-SIZED HAUL BAG, AFFEC-
TIONATELY CALLED THE "PIG" AND THREE
CLIMBERS. EVERYTHING, INCLUDING THE
CLIMBER IS UNDER TENSION.

On Brad's lead of the next pitch, he pendulumed across a 30-foot blank section of the wall to a large dihedral—a feature similar to an inside corner of an attached buttress on a granite church, only this one was 600 feet (two football fields) above the ground. It was the first time any of us had moved really fluidly on the rock. To complete this and any pendulum pitch, the second climber straddles the haul bag and rides it across before he ascends the haul line. John followed separately to the base of the dihedral, where he cleaned the gear Brad had placed and climbed up the tied-off lead line. If this process reads like it is very complex, then the nearly three hours this one pitch consumed confirms the reality on the cliff. We had budgeted two hours.

When Brad noted our pace that morning was again slow, he grew skeptical as to our likelihood of success. John felt the onset of an ordeal and found himself in a position where his willpower failed to help him overcome the psychological burdens of this climb.

As I climbed the bolt ladder (a series of bolts and hangers drilled into otherwise featureless rock) above Dolt Hole, I should have been fit and gutsy enough to "Batman" or hand-over-hand climb each stickus's reach, but my efforts devolved to tedious bolt-to-bolt aid climbing, much like my performance on my previous lead. What should have taken minutes, took tens of minutes. My confidence eroded further as we only had enough food and water for a faster ascent. A hollowness grew in my stomach as I realized that failure was increasingly likely.

The second half of this pitch involved the most dynamic actions by the leader yet. Surmounting the bolt ladder, I clipped the rope through a carabiner attached to the highest bolt, from which I was lowered 60 feet down to a point just lower than the Dolt Hole belay station. From my low point, I cast off running, first left, away from my objective, the Stovelegs Crack, then back right, hurdling the edge of the dihedral, running hard for the crack which was out of sight to my right.

Fifteen feet shy after my first running pendulum effort, I reversed and sprinted sideways across the cliff, leaping off the dihedral and running as high as I could. Temporarily hesitating at my leftward apogee, I dug hard right, hurdling again and continued digging. Nearing the crack, I dove sideways and stabbed a camming device in the crack and stopped cold.

I had never before swung deliberately on a cliff 700 feet up, and certainly never ran at full speed to reach a hand hold. Up to that point, the *Nose* forced a snail's pace and leg-numbing hanging belays. My mobility on this pitch was the highlight of the climb so far.

"How's it look?" They intoned, once it was clear I wasn't going to skitter into their field of view again.

There now existed, for the first time, a physical separation of our team that eroded the emotional support of proximity. The Stovelegs Crack ended ten feet below me, revealing 700 feet of unblemished, sheer granite. Above me, a continuous crack soared 400 feet directly up the face to Dolt Tower—a patio-sized ledge at the top of pitch 12. I couldn't see Brad or John behind the edge of the dihedral.

"I'm in the crack now, and it looks climbable, but I won't be able to protect till I get above the pendulum point—about 50 feet. I am going to leap-frog some gear. It is going to take a while," I shouted back, breathlessly. Since I had been lowered 60 feet I had to re-lead the pitch in the parallel crack. I climbed the crack steadily.

SICKLE LEDGE TO STOVELEGS CRACK ENTAILS TWO PENDULUMS. THE WHITE CIRCLE MARKS HAUL BAGS BEING RAISED FROM SICKLE LEDGE. WHITE "X"s MARK BELAY STATIONS. BASE TO TOP THIS IMAGE SHOWS 400 OF EL CAPITAN'S 3,000 FEET.

From Brad and John's position they could not see the progress I was making on this pitch, but discussed our overall progress.

"At this rate we won't get to El Cap Tower till 10 at night. We'll be spent tomorrow," Brad realistically analyzed. He felt overwhelmed by the logistics, was scared of the height, and knew we were so far behind schedule that our food and water would never hold out, even if our constitutions did. He was distraught. He rarely misjudges to the extent that failure results.

"I'm scared, and out of my league. The exposure is sickening and I am really unsure about how to retreat. The higher we go the worse I feel," John willingly confessed.

Our lack of progress and obvious underestimation of the difficulty of this route made it clear we wouldn't succeed. They made the group's decision to retreat. John's relief would be permanent, as this climb had found for him the limits of his willpower. Brad knew the conditions were not right, and considered our retreat temporary.

JOHN AND BRAD WERE TOGETHER AT THE DOLT HOLE WHERE THEY MADE THE DECISION FOR OUR TEAM TO RETREAT. THE TEAM WAS TOO SLOW, NOT SUFFICIENTLY FIT, SCARED OF THE HEIGHT AND UNCERTAIN ABOUT THE EASE OF DESCENT. FIVE DAYS ON EL CAPITAN WAS AN OVERWHELMING PROSPECT.

"Lead rope fixed! Hauling rope ready, go ahead and lower out the bags," I called from above after reaching the belay.

"Bruce is going to want to continue," said John to Brad, sensing my enthusiasm and energy.

"We are a team and two of us say we go down, that's the risk he takes," rationalized Brad.

"I'll follow the lead line and tell him," said Brad. "You ride the bags across and wait for us to rappel down."

John straddled the pig and lowered himself across. Brad followed the lead rope up to the pendulum point and lowered himself sideways till he was below my position, from where he jümared straight up.

"We decided at the last belay to go down. At this pace we will never make it," Brad announced.

I received the news with mixed emotions. A majority had called for retreat—a convenient alibi for me. Eight hundred feet of exposure gave me a sickening feeling when I stopped long enough to consider it. It was easy for me to say we could keep going till a few hours before dark, and maybe sleep on Dolt Tower.

There was no discussion. Cameras came out to record our high point. We lightened the haul bag by dropping all non-breakables, watching them tumble and drift to the ground. Ironically, when we poured out our water, it evaporated in the withering afternoon heat before it even hit the ground.

Our fears and uncertainty, sustained as we rappelled down featureless granite, were finally

**JOHN DUMPS THE TEAM'S WATER OUT BEFORE RAPPELLING. IT EVAPORATED BEFORE REACHING THE GROUND.**

relieved when we reached the ground around 5pm. There, I struggled with mounting frustration and shame. I was pensive and still harbored mixed feelings about Brad and John's decision. We avoided words beyond those necessary as we gathered our wind-scattered gear. There was an underlying current of embarrassment. Our failure had happened so early in the climb and so quickly. We were now looking at cooling our heels in Yosemite for a week before our flights back to Denver. While collecting our furthest straying gear, Brad reported a six-foot wide half-circle of blood on the base of the wall—icing the cake of our decision to bail.

I phoned my parents and girlfriend to relieve them of concern for our safety and to reluctantly admit that we had called it off. I heard support from my parents, but I stubbornly could not accept it because I had failed in my mission.

I had an easy scapegoat in John and Brad. I could point to their decision and leave unexplored what my reaction would have been had it been me at the belay in Dolt Hole. Despite our commonly held fear and uncertainty of climbing higher, I remained frustrated that we did not seek a higher limit. Why stop when there was food, gear and daylight left and no weather threat? My frustration stemmed from my failure to discern that personal

FRUSTRATED, YET RELIEVED THE AUTHOR SITS AT THE BASE OF EL CAPITAN FOLLOWING HIS FAILED ATTEMPT IN 1991.

allegiances and historical friendships may impede goal achievement. Yet my inexperience would not have allowed me to successfully find other partner options in the same time frame. So while at times personally disappointed with my decisions, circumstances effectively dictated the outcome far in advance of our attempt. It would take time and greater maturity to understand this reality and act accordingly.

Upon our return to Denver, John rechanneled his energies into business, personal relationships and less-scary sports. Brad and I continued to chip away at our adventure checklists. Deluding ourselves into failure on El Capitan impeded the historical fluidity of our relationships. I found it more difficult to talk of, or plan, the "next greater" adventure with Brad and John. The rose-colored-glasses through which our abilities seemed equal before had been wiped clear.

The next summer I moved to Arizona for work. I felt like I had been pushed from the nest as most of my recreational and social friends remained in Denver. But, I stayed in touch with Brad and found him yearning to resume our climb on El Capitan. We agreed to attempt the *Nose* again in the summer of 1993.

This time my training was uninterrupted by work or social concerns. A typical weekday's training routine would entail running five miles, 200 push-ups and 400 sit-ups done at lunch. This was followed after work by mountain biking and indoor climbing. Later in the evenings, I would lift weights in my garage "gym" and simulate aid climbing using webbing straps hung from the rafters. I handled concrete blocks and walked barefoot on my asphalt shingle roof to build callus. Weekends generally found me with no partners who could match my training regime, so I solo climbed (albeit with a rope) as many routes as I could each day. The only weakness in my preparation was failing to find routes with El Capitan-like exposure. I trained with a single-minded passion knowing now the full commitment required for success on the *Nose*.

Brad's effort to prepare was hampered by two events—a new relationship and the separate deaths of two climbing-partner friends. Both climbing unroped, one perished climbing ice and the other on rock. These deaths, had they occurred while roped, would have compelled Brad to stop rock climbing altogether. While his physical training was dedicated and sufficient, peripheral psychological barriers remained.

By April 1993, the logistics for our resumed attempt on the *Nose* began to take shape. My brother, Steve, would come to California to be our support crew. Brad and I planned to warm up on *Freeblast,* a 10-pitch El Capitan route, early in the week,

THE *AIGUILLE DE JOSH*, OR THE NEEDLE OF JOSHUA TREE, CALIFORNIA, ON WHICH THE AUTHOR IS PICTURED ABOVE, WAS A TYPICAL ADVENTURE WHILE HE LIVED IN ARIZONA.

followed by a day's rest before a five-day push on the *Nose*. Limiting our party to two people would lessen the risk of failure and lighten our haul bag. I was prepared to put all of my efforts into achieving my goal—submitting again to fear, uncertainty and previously unheard of levels of training. I believed we would succeed.

The week before we were scheduled to meet in Yosemite, word spread through the climbing community that the famous Colorado climber, Derek Hersey, had been killed while unroped solo climbing on Sentinel Rock in Yosemite. Brad knew Derek from years of giving him rides between Boulder and Eldorado Canyon. I had met him once or twice. This death, so physically and temporally proximal to our climb, had a huge mental effect on Brad.

The day before Brad left for Yosemite, he typed a note to his girlfriend and family, expressing his love and willing his climbing gear. He asked a co-worker to open the computer file should he not return. I was unaware of the impact these events had on Brad's psyche and blissfully continued my preparations 700 miles away.

Snow above 6,000 feet greeted us as we approached Yosemite Valley. From the misty roadside meadow at the base of El Capitan we craned our necks to look up at the mile-and-a-half wide by two-thirds-of-a-mile high expanse of granite. It loomed over us like the bow of a supertanker to a swimmer. I was once again struck by the *Nose's* immensity and prominence. Its bold thrust challenged me. My desire to climb it remained unchanged.

That day, El Capitan was bathed in water below half-height and crusted above in wet snow to its crown, making it unclimbable for a few days. Fortunately, the forecast called for progressively improving weather. Steve, Brad and I walked through the incense cedar, live oak and massive Douglas fir trees to the base of the wall to get reacquainted with the approach and first pitches.

**EL CAPITAN'S OVERHANGING UPPER WALL STREAKED FROM MELTING SNOW. JUNE 1993.**

We found a sheet of frigid water a quarter-inch thick streaming down the wall. We could make out climbers in their portaledges nearly a third of a mile straight above us on the *Shield* route. It must have been unpleasant up there suffering through what we would learn had been a five-day wind, rain and snow storm. Looking the opposite way along the base, we saw a grisly scene—the scattered contents of a climbing team's haul bag—evidence of a failed attempt. There was the bag itself—split open with numerous carabiners, chocks, camming devices, clothing and sleeping bags scattered amongst the talus. This sight brought back memories of our jettisoned gear in 1991.

One rope-length above us, two men rappelled down from the *Nose*. Figuring to help them out, we collected their scattered gear. Our walk took us past the site where the blood stained half-circle had been two years before. The harsh realities of this wall were in our faces once again.

When the descending climbers reached the ground, we saw that they had pinched faces that contrasted their nearly twice-normal-sized swollen hands—as if they had been in a bathtub for days. Neither man could untie their rope. After helping them, we pointed to the pile of their gear we had collected. They spilled their story.

"We started five days ago, and after two days got to El Cap Towers where the storm trapped us," said the first climber. "My hands were so numb that I dropped the haul bag on the first rappel this morning."

Eight consecutive rappels were needed to reach the ground from their bivouac on El Cap Towers, 1,200 feet up. They didn't need to elaborate. Their haul bag reached terminal velocity and impacted the ground with devastating force. Digesting this unsettling news, we probed for other information and learned stunning news: instead of dumping their water as we had in 1991, they left eight gallons on El Cap Tower. At a one gallon per-person-per-day summertime ration, this would save us 65 pounds if we could count on it.

"Can we ask a favor of you guys?" I anxiously queried. "Don't tell anyone else about the water."

They looked at us curiously, slowly seeing our angle. "We're out of here today. We won't say anything," they agreed.

BRAD APPROACHES THE BASE OF EL CAPITAN CARRYING OUR HAUL BAG. THE TOP CURVE OF SICKLE LEDGE, WHERE THE AUTHOR TRAVERSED WITHOUT A ROPE IS VISIBLE AT CENTER LEFT. ON EL CAP TOWERS, HALFWAY UP EL CAPITAN, VISIBLE IMMEDIATELY LEFT OF THE TREE BRANCHES, WE EXPECTED TO FIND EIGHT GALLONS OF WATER LEFT BY A PREVIOUS PARTY.

Saving three days worth of water weight in our haul bag would increase our speed and improve our odds. Smug with our knowledge, we headed off to prepare our gear for when the weather cleared.

Rain and 45°F temperatures oppressed us again the next day. Our plan to climb *Freeblast* as a warm-up was shelved. I was pensive and expectant. I itched to climb, anxious that my hard-won fitness would erode. I wondered if we were going to suffer from the same issues we did two years before.

YOSEMITE FALLS, A 1,000-FOOT CAS-
CADE A SHORT WAY UP-VALLEY FROM EL
CAPITAN, FUELED BY RECENT RAINS.

The bad weather had also delayed Spanish, German and California teams. By 10am the next day, however, it was clear and warming—60°F temperatures and clear skies were forecast for the week. We planned to stage to Sickle Ledge, much like we had done before.

The Germans and Spaniards were first on the wall that morning. We started only minutes before one of the California team got started (his partner was to catch up later that evening). Our progress up the first three pitches was much smoother and faster than our 1991 attempt. On the second pitch the Californian asked to use our ropes which we were leaving in place as part of our first day's staging. We were familiar with the route and confident enough to share our labors with a stranger. We agreed that his partner could ascend our ropes to Sickle Ledge later that night.

Brad was efficient, but cautious and pensive. I was bold, fast and nearly fearless on my leads. It was on the fourth pitch that the difference between Brad's and my psychological states was vocalized.

"Bruce, you are sick. I would never have trusted that," Brad said as he unhooked a carabiner of ours from a rusty and bent piton that pivoted in its crack when I had weighted it. We both knew the piton had been there two years before and likely for decades before that. Placing my own protection would add marginal safety, but eat up valuable time. My risk pendulum swung towards pace over safety, while Brad's settled somewhere in the center. My attitude was: *go fast, trust the gear or go home.* I wasn't going home empty-handed this time.

Our plan to stage again to Sickle Ledge and return to the base to eat and sleep before resuming the next morning caused a dilemma. Our ropes were deliberately left fixed on the first four pitches. We planned to use another party's ropes to rappel from the center of Sickle Ledge, 50 feet away. To bridge the gap I chose to walk, unroped, across the four-foot wide ledge, despite a sheer drop of 450 feet. Brad was visibly upset by my recklessness, for here was his partner for the next four days behaving in the same manner that recently killed three of his friends.

Within two hours we had rappelled to the ground, met up with Steve, and made our way to the pizza joint in Yosemite Village. Once there, Brad requested I accompany him outside for a private conversation.

"I have deliberated about this. I can't do it. I've had a premonition that I would die up there. And, seeing you clip that old piton and solo across Sickle Ledge freaked me out. If I forced myself to go up I would ultimately make us turn around," he said.

I was caught unprepared. My investment was so substantial physically and mentally that I snapped, "What am I going to do now?" I felt like the rug was pulled out from under me.

Brad suffered because he too felt the disappointment. Brad was a great climbing partner, but not now on this climb. My vision was narrowed to my selfish goal, and I had forgotten that to rock climb a multi-pitch big wall route takes two people at similar physical and mental states.

One second I felt relieved because Brad had given me an out again, and the next I was sorely disappointed and shamed again for having overinvested in a risky proposition. My physical and mental preparation was complete, but I was still intimidated by the immensity of the wall and therefore was susceptible to temptations to avoid following through with the climb.

Brad wasn't going to let me back out if he could help it. He suggested a rare and unique option, "I think that Californian guy we helped would take you on as a partner. Without our ropes they would not be on Sickle Ledge and ready to go for tomorrow."

If my intent was real, it should not matter with whom I climbed, just that I did the climb. All I had to do was ascend our ropes the next morning and ask two Californians I hardly knew and who knew nothing of me. The chances of being taken in were slim. I had little to lose by trying.

Relief changed to dread as my mental state regressed to a pit-in-the-stomach feeling I got from knowing that with another team I might be pushed further than I would have with Brad. If accepted, I would have to keep up and contribute.

That night I reorganized my gear and packed up food despite the foreboding feeling of committing to a highly uncertain process and outcome.

Rising before my alarm, there was faint light in the east when my brother and Brad got up to see me jümar back up to Sickle Ledge. I barely got there in time to make an offer at all. The Californians had already started and were nearly out of earshot on the far end of Sickle Ledge.

I called across the gap, "Hello! Good Morning, it's Bruce, one of the guys whose ropes you used yesterday. My partner bailed. Are you guys willing to take on a third person?" I was selling an untested product, so I continued, "I have done the first eight pitches before and am in wicked good shape. I can do all of the hauling if necessary."

I threw in that bone having seen one of them struggle the day before. They discussed something briefly.

"Where are you from?" They asked.

"Soon to be Colorado," I replied, as I was moving back to Denver the following week.

They discussed something else.

"OK, my wife's family is from Evergreen, Colorado. We'll take you on," Michael, the second climber, called over.

Where I lived and how it related to Michael's wife's family seemed unimportant to me. What I thought should be important was my ability and desire. I wondered what motivated them to take me on.

The two Californians were divinity college friends and accomplished 5.12 climbers with an ascent of Half Dome's *Northwest Face* under their belts. Michael Trostrud was a Baptist minister from a nearby California foothills town on four days leave before he had to return to preach. Tom Broxson, a geography graduate student at the time, lived in Corvallis, Oregon, and was on his first major climb since recovering from a near-fatal fall on the *Prow* on Yosemite's *Washington Column* the year before. Tom fell 200 feet, broke ankles, wrists, an upper arm, suffered a concussion and was plucked from the cliff face by a rescue helicopter. His fractures healed, but his climbing confidence was still mending. Climbing El Capitan was to be his first major post-accident climb.

Their climbing backgrounds were similar to mine—progressively harder climbs of renown, or classic, climbs. Their academic aspirations and resulting careers, like mine, prevented full-time dedication to climbing and adventuring. Therefore, on this day in June, we were all average Joe-climbers out on crusades.

I felt obligated to explain that I had brought only one day's worth of water. If the stash of water was not on El Cap Towers (three days had passed since I learned about the water), I would have to descend, taking two of the teams' three ropes, which would force everyone to descend. They were going to have to take my word and have faith. Paradoxically, my confident treatment of this risky complication revealed to them my "all or nothing" attitude. By not changing their minds about my joining them because of my "lack of baggage," they had cast their lot with mine.

I took a deep breath, closed my eyes briefly, grateful for acceptance, and thought of my last chance to bail off the route. I was going to join with two unknown people who, evidenced by their quick acceptance of me, were apparently as rash and impulsive as I—a psychological match. This truth was scary, and it was also just what I needed to achieve a goal that was of a significantly-higher standard than any I had sought before.

I threw the two ropes I had carried for my own retreat (if I was not accepted) to the talus 450 feet below, signaling to Brad and Steve that I was going to test my convictions.

Easing into a rhythm and finding ourselves accepting the same level of risk, we succeeded in making Dolt Tower (pitch 12) by late afternoon. We were neither fast nor ethically pure climbers that day. I used the stickus on occasion. Michael made jokes about the ancient aluminum bolts we were trusting at the belays. I could laugh along with the jokes, but not make them myself, for I was conserving my mental energy for the climb. Michael, being a man of God, also joked about the heavy haul bag—his "burden."

At one point, just below Dolt Tower, the Stovelegs Crack expanded to about a foot wide and got sharply harder to climb. A rope trailed down from the Spanish party just ahead. "¿Puedo jümar su cuerda," I asked. "Si," came the reply. Success over style. After Dolt Tower, we made our way up the three easier pitches leading to El Cap Towers where the critical water should have been waiting.

It was nearly dark when we arrived. On the ledge where the water was supposed to be only Germans and Spaniards snored. Final word on the water would have to wait till morning. I slept fitfully on a three- by five-foot sloping ledge, knowing a negative response on water would mean team failure.

At first light, when I heard movement above, I called up to the Germans and Spaniards asking about the water. "Nein . No!" came down. "What?" I asked again, trying to be clearer, but got the same answer. I was devastated. That was it, we would have to retreat. I had risked it all, put in a huge effort over the last two days, and just because I pushed into their group, Tom and Michael would have to retreat also. I felt awful and could barely look them in the eye.

**Michael Trostrud on pitch 7 of El Capitan's *Nose*.**

Michael couldn't believe that the other teams might have consumed six gallons of extra water if they had carried up full rations. He climbed up to the top ledge of the Towers where he actually saw that "no" meant: "No, we didn't drink it all." Four gallons remained. Two gallons for me and two for Tom and Michael—who now needed the water because we were moving much slower than they had projected. We all relaxed.

The rigors of jümaring and aid climbing caused Tom and Michael's feet to become so swollen that they winced in pain with each step that morning. Tom had naively envisioned free climbing the *Nose* in his tight-fitting sport climbing shoes, underestimating the difficulties of space hauling, heavy aid racks, exposure, hanging belays and jümaring on his climbing ability and body parts. My feet were armored by the second rand layer I had glued around the toe box on my shoes and toughened from the seemingly crazy roof walking I did in Phoenix. Our hands were sore, but manageable as we had taped them or used fingerless gloves.

Just as we were starting to climb, a climber we had not seen pulled up on the last moves and mantled on to our ledge.

"Good morning," he said. With only a sweater around his waist, one waterbottle and a couple of energy bars in his pocket this guy was traveling light.

**TOM BROXSON ON EL CAP TOWER.**
**"MY FEET, CAN YOU SAY PAIN?"**

"Trying it in a day?" I casually asked, trying to veil my awe.

He and his partner had started at 3am and now, four hours later, were at pitch 15—a distance that had taken us two days. Despite the cheating and begging I had employed to get me this far, I had been feeling pretty good about my abilities. But, here, in my face, was evidence that fitness and one's opinion of acceptable risk varied all over the map. After nearly ten years of climbing, I knew that there was no chance for me to climb with the fluidity and freedom I saw these men carry off. Maybe it was time for me to find a different sport that would allow me to achieve their level of finesse.

Our tired and pained team packed the new supply of water and set off. Michael led Texas Flake—named for its Lone Star State shape—by chimnying (feet on one wall, back to the other) the unprotected gap between the detached flake and the main wall. A jagged rock pile at the suture with the main wall would arrest him if he fell from his body-wedge position. The rumors that circulated amongst aspiring *Nose* climbers was that rats fed off of bodies of climbers who fell from this chimney into the jagged rocks. I hoped Michael relished the lead—for I envied the bragging rights he earned by cheating the rats.

Tom aided a subsequent bolt ladder that led to a 5.10 difficulty fist-sized crack along the edge of Boot Flake—so named because of its distinctive boot shape. From its top, I was lowered for the double pendulum King Swing, which led to the base of two pitches of discontinuous cracks through the only loose and fractured part of cliff. Contrasting the tightly-scripted moves of the rest of the climb, the mobility of the pendulums was short lived. Immediately after the King Swing, the crack climbing became difficult and stressful.

Our pace slowed. Halfway through Michael's lead of the next pitch, our fourth of the day, it was 2pm. A pace of ten pitches per day must be kept if Michael was to keep his job. Furthermore, our water supplies now matched Michael's schedule. At our pace we would have to climb 15 hours per day. We were collectively daunted by our predicament, but didn't change our tactics, because we were each going as fast as we safely could.

After I led the 21st pitch, which topped out just below Camp Four, I tied off the haul line. Michael rode the pigs over in one 300-pound package. As he jümared the haul line, his arm and foot action caused the taught rope to abrade against a sharp edge ten feet below me. I saw that it would be only moments before the sheath cut, exposing to its core Michael's only connection to

THE AUTHOR BELAYS MICHAEL TROS-TRUD FROM THE HIGHEST LEDGE OF EL CAP TOWERS AS MICHAEL CHIMNEYS BEHIND TEXAS FLAKE.

the cliff. Despite being 1,800 feet off the ground, I unclipped from the belay, soloed easy ground to the sharp edge and padded the abrasion point with one of my kneepads. Michael chuckled knowingly as he watched. We were a team.

Concerns over water rationing and unemployment spurred us to climb into the night. Abetting our speed effort, I found pitons were already in place across the crack at the junction between the vertical cliff and the "eaves" of the Great Roof. Headlamp illuminating my path, I reached from piton to piton with the stickus, moving with a nearly simian rhythm, making the belay faster than any of us expected. Tom released the lower end of the lead rope, which I pulled through, sacrificing four carabiners. This gambit spared Tom having to follow the horizontal line the lead rope had taken through those carabiners, for jümaring sideways out the underside of the roof would have been tedious and time consuming. I would rappel directly back to the ledges, taking the direct line instead of the up and out line of the roof feature. The team would ascend the rappel line in the morning. I felt a slight confidence surge as I started to arrange the rappel.

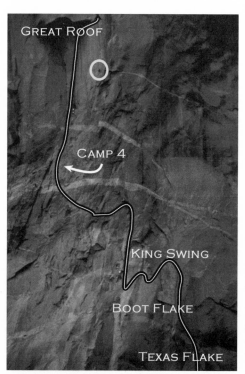

THE TEAM'S SLOWEST SECTION - TEXAS FLAKE (BOTTOM RIGHT) TO THE GREAT ROOF. THE ROUTE IS INDICATED BY THE OVERLAIN LINE. INSIDE THE CIRCLE IS ANOTHER TEAM'S HAUL BAG.

I tied the rope to three bolts at the belay station, dropped the rope's other end straight down and saw that it hung 40 feet sideways from the Camp Four ledges where Tom and Michael waited. I would have to pendulum from the bottom of the rope to make camp. Rappelling a single line 2,000 feet off the ground scared me. I pulled up the loose end, tied off a loop and clipped it back to my harness so that there was no way I could rappel off the end of the rope. The uncertainty of being in a space I had never before experienced made me nervous and less coordinated. As I descended, the rope snaked through my figure eight rappel device, hardly giving me enough friction, adding to my mental and physical tension. I gripped the rope tightly to stay in control, but felt it twisting strangely in my hands. Suddenly the rope snarled and I was stuck, dangling in space 40 feet above and 40 feet to the side of where Tom and Michael relaxed.

I was forced to unclip the safety knot so the twist spun free. Resuming, I descended to the end of the rope, where I gripped its knotted end tightly and commenced penduluming. Like the other pendulums, I had to first run away from my objective and then sprint hard back towards it. This time fear, darkness and occupied hands compounded the difficulty of the exercise. First try, I tripped, spun out of control and smashed, helmet first into a dihedral. Slowed down now, I clambered across the rock back to where I started. Collecting my wits like a cartoon character, I refocused on my goal, kept my footing and finally succeeded in reaching my partners. After this episode I remained shaken and slightly less confident in my ability to function alone in the dark. The optimism of moments before had been gnawed at.

That night at Camp Four, I slept partially suspended in a web of rope on a desk-sized, slightly-sloping (outward) ledge. Tom and Michael shared a similarly abbreviated ledge.

Before dawn, we sequentially jümared to the top of the Great Roof via my rappel line fixed the night before. We were all tired, had hands more swollen and sore than the day before and Tom's feet were now blistered and bleeding. Foot pain forced Michael to switch from his climbing shoes to a pair of comfortable approach shoes, further reducing our climbing speed. Tom did not have the luxury of an extra pair of shoes and suffered an acute erosion of his leading ability. On the next pitch, Pancake Flake—named for the width of the rock flake one ascends—Tom struggled to free climb 5.10 difficulty rock, two grades below his normal ability.

We were 2,500 feet above ground by late afternoon. That day we had thrashed upward, suffering falls and route-finding difficulties on the awkward cracks and dihedrals of the pitches above the Great Roof. The exposure was stupefying. Our position was equivalent to being clipped to the outside of a window on the top of two stacked Empire State Buildings. Peregrine falcons and sparrows whizzed by, only feet from our belay stations. I wished for their ease of mobility. With each additional pitch, we projected slightly further out over the valley floor. The summit was obscured.

The conditions we found at Camp Five and Camp Six reflected the psychology of climbers at this height. Feces and urine infest the cracks and ledges. Defecation has to be done in plain sight of your partners at uncomfortably close quarters. Parties with poor aim unwittingly bombed or showered climbers below. Dehumanization prevailed.

It seemed that nothing mattered at this height. For us too, progress upward became a selfish "get me to the top at all costs" activity.

We arrived in Camp Six around 9pm. It was a cave-like, dripping wet, smelly and garbage covered corner-table-sized platform. Above it, the cliff was in shadow and our only light came from a narrow view down valley. Our pace again had been too slow that day to keep us on the schedule dictated by Michael's job and our water supply. Michael bemoaned the fact that he would probably lose his job. We finished the last of our water.

THE UPPER THIRD OF EL CAP REARS FROM THE LEDGES OF CAMP 4 THROUGH THE STEEPENING DIHEDRALS ABOVE THE GREAT ROOF TO THE FINAL SUMMIT OVERHANG.

We were compelled to push for the summit that night. Having caught up to the Germans at Camp Six, we learned that they too were on final rations. Michael, our strongest leader, teamed with the German party. He and they alternated leads over the last six pitches, leaving Tom and me to follow. My strength remained, but, by this point, the exposure and darkness and sleep deprivation started taking its toll on my mental stability and ability to function.

On each successive pitch, Tom would assuage my fears while we waited together. With his help, I willed my way through my mounting fear of the height and overhang. The cliff leaned out over the valley now. There was more air than rock under my feet. I no longer had the guts nor the mental drive to be a leader or seek the bravado pitches. I felt comfortable merely following. I accepted the fact that making the top was going to be achieved increasingly through other's efforts.

When it was my turn to ascend first I was only alone during the time I jümared the rope, for I left Tom at the bottom and usually found a German climber at the top. When it was my turn to go second, I became prone to self-doubt and debilitating fear while I waited alone as Tom moved into the dark above. I was operating in a shadowy world backed up by a massive black void. An irrational fear grew in me despite stable conditions and days of proof that our system and equipment worked.

What was different? It was the exposure and the growing fear of being in an uncomfortable and unnatural space. It was like driving too fast in a car. You had some control, but inside you knew that you were in a space that could become unstable and kill you. Having never been so high off the ground before, I had no experience on which to draw to help guide me through my natural fears of the setting.

From this position of overwhelming exposure I reflected on my motivation to continue to rock climb at this level. I had found the training too solitary for my taste, and now, as I remembered the thirty or so pitches I had ascended over the past four days, I realized that I had actually only lead eight of them. And of those, on only two did I do any free climbing that allowed fluidity of motion. My mind kept slipping to an experience I had had a week before on my first whitewater kayak trip. Kayaking required less energy for comparable thrills.

**TOM, 11PM, SUMMIT PUSH.**

As it grew dark, the trees in the valley, which had begun to look like blades of grass, faded from view. We were in a separate reality. It had taken us four days to reach this point. The same amount of time it could take to drive across the country. Self sufficiency and determination were the tools we relied on to escape our isolation.

The first three of the last four pitches overhang vertically 10 feet for every 100 feet. The last pitch overhangs nearly 30 feet. The final climber encounters a minimum 30-foot separation from the cliff and a 60-foot swing if he is unable to lower himself out slowly.

The moon rose over Half Dome. We had been climbing about 16 hours already that day. Tom and I were at the base of the last pitch. It was Tom's turn to go first. The rope he ascended was fixed to the summit tree and to our belay, so his ascent followed a controlled line parallel to the overhanging cliff. After he moved out of sight, I was left alone nearly 3,000 feet straight above the valley floor. It would be a half hour before his call from the dark above would release me from this forced solitude.

My headlamp batteries had died long ago. I looked west and I saw a shadow on the cliff about 50 feet away in the shape of a sitting man. My heart went into my throat. I believed I saw the ghost of Derek Hersey. Maybe Brad's premonition was right. Or contrarily, maybe Derek was there to support our effort. I turned away, genuinely scared and uncertain. The effects of sleep deprivation had set in.

I was tethered by a length of webbing to three bolts. My feet rested on a three-inch wide ledge. I could not balance without holding on to the cliff-end of my tether because the wall overhung. I fought sleep as I waited for my signal to ascend. When sleep overcame me, I would lose my hand grip, slump down to the limit of my tether, jerk awake, stand up again, only to repeat this unnerving process moments later. If I was a dog I would have whimpered. I was failing to maintain focus on my objective. My experience bank was overdrawn. I didn't know how to temper my growing fear.

Tom yelled down, "Rope is fixed, climb away!" I jerked fully awake. My adrenaline surged.

I looked down. I saw the a car creep soundlessly along the Merced River road. The moon had just risen over Half Dome. Tom was out of sight above.

I tightened up my jümars on the rope that curved down from the dark above, trying to get as much slack out of the system as possible before I unclipped from the belay. I used the tail generated from pulling the slack to lower out and minimize the swing, but, after ten feet, my slack was used up. I steeled my nerves for one last time before I cast off into space. My stomach tightened, my fear level crested as I accelerated down and then out through about a 50-foot arc. G-forces tore at my stomach.

Swinging into space, there was no rock at my feet to reassure. I relied on the rope and my harness alone for connection to reality.

As the oscillation lessened, I settled into a determined inner space that I had found time and time again as a competitive ski racer. I mechanically ascended the rope. At each rest point I paused to appreciate the setting. Despite my fear, I realized this free-hanging jümar was a once-in-a-lifetime experience. These were my last moments on the *Nose*. Years of training, built-up expectations and risks had come down to this climax. I was going to make it.

Three minutes of jümaring later and I was on top! There was no cheering or backslapping. The only sound was the rustling of sore hands digging in the haul bag for sleeping bags.

The moon and stars witnessed the achievement of my goal. I didn't need others to give value to my accomplishment. I would look back on this success and forever know the limit of my rock climbing capabilities.

BRAD AND STEVE HIKED IN OVERNIGHT AND, WITH TOM AND MICHAEL'S WIVES, JOINED US FOR A SUMMIT CELEBRATION. WE WERE ON TOP OF THE WORLD THAT DAY.

FIRST THING I DID ON RETURN TO CIVILIZATION WAS CALL MY PARENTS TO RELATE MY SUCCESS AND HEAR THEIR RELIEF. I ALSO FINALLY UNDERSTOOD THE ADMIRATION MY FATHER HELD FOR ME ALL ALONG.

FIGURING OUT MY DAD APPRECIATED ME ALL ALONG MIGHT HAVE CAUSED ME TO CEASE TRYING TO PROVE MYSELF TO SOMEONE ELSE, BUT MY INNER DRIVE TO CHALLENGE MYSELF REMAINED. FOLLOWING EL CAPITAN, I MOVED ON FROM ONE EXTREME SPORT TO ANOTHER—FROM CLIMBING STATIONARY ROCK TO KAYAKING IN EVER FASTER WATER.

MICHAEL TROSTRUD, TOM BROXSON AND THE AUTHOR SAVOR THE SUMMIT OF EL CAPITAN, JUNE 11, 1993.

Torrey Carroll

Survive while you gain ability and judgement on the extreme rivers of the Sierra Nevada and you find a wealth of adventure waiting. Todd Dickson on last drop before Atom Bomb Falls, Middle Fork Feather River—Bald Rock Canyon Section, July 2001.

# California's Clavey River

*"...irrational exuberance..."*
—Alan Greenspan

## HARD CORE RECALIBRATION

IN THE FALL OF 1996, I TRADED A SECURE SOCIAL SETTING FOR AMBITION. I MOVED FROM DENVER TO SACRAMENTO, WHERE MY NEW JOB WAS TO RUN A TALC PROCESSING PLANT AND MINE. I DID SOME ROCK CLIMBING, MOUNTAINEERING AND SURFING IN MY ADOPTED STATE, BUT PRIMARILY I PADDLED MY WHITEWATER KAYAK. I RAN MY FIRST CALIFORNIA CLASS 5 RIVER—THE NORTH FORK OF THE STANISLAUS—WHERE I WAS INTRODUCED TO A SMALL GROUP OF KAYAKERS WHO REGULARLY RAN DIFFICULT RIVERS SUCH AS THE CHERRY CREEK SECTION OF THE TUOLUMNE RIVER OUTSIDE OF YOSEMITE. IMBUED WITH POST-EL CAPITAN CONFIDENCE, I WAS NOT AFRAID TO VENTURE OUT WITH ATHLETES I DIDN'T KNOW PERSONALLY AS I SOUGHT TO FIND MY NICHE IN THIS COMMUNITY AND SATISFY MY DESIRE FOR ADVENTURE.

Spring runoff was just beginning and my kayaking juices were starting to flow. So when I received the phone call on a Friday night in March, I was primed.

"Bruce, it's Dieter King." I had recently bought a used kayak from Dieter, but had never paddled with him, so his call was a bit of a surprise. Dieter was an elite kayaker, known throughout California for his first descents of extreme rivers.

"Lee Wilhelm and I are kayaking the upper and lower Clavey this weekend. Wanna come with? It's an overnight trip—first day easier and second harder. The flow is around 700 cfs—a good introductory level," he said.

I thought, "Lee Wilhelm!" He was another character of nearly mythical reputation. Campfire lore set him on a pedestal for his solo descents of California Class 5 test piece rivers. I was a rank beginner compared to these kayakers.

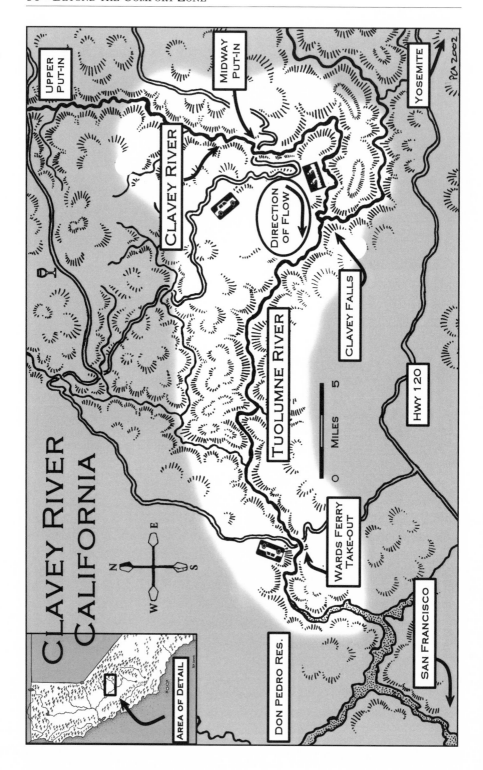

CLAVEY RIVER
CALIFORNIA

UPPER PUT-IN

MIDWAY PUT-IN

YOSEMITE

CLAVEY RIVER

DIRECTION OF FLOW

CLAVEY FALLS

TUOLUMNE RIVER

HWY 120

MILES
0   5

WARDS FERRY TAKE-OUT

DON PEDRO RES.

SAN FRANCISCO

AREA OF DETAIL

N E S W

*The Best Whitewater in California* by Stanley and Holbeck describes the 20-mile long Clavey River as "…a stretch that no high gradient/low volume enthusiast should miss." Two miles of 170-foot-per-mile whitewater cap its 137-fpm average gradient. Typical of guidebooks for the cutting-edge adventurer, this description of the Clavey River held no detail, just generalizations about an unrelenting series of Class 5+ drops, innumerable portages and no egress except by water. This river was serious, even for the cognoscienti.

Though I was unsure why he had called me, I was enchanted by my first invitation to paddle a big-league river. I had not yet paddled a river as difficult as the Clavey. Having only scratched the surface of the upper end of kayaking's classes, I asked the typical questions of a not-quite-Class 5+ boater considering stepping way out of his comfort zone.

"Can the teeth be portaged?"

"Yes," Dieter responded.

"How many times have you run this river?" I asked, knowing the more familiar they were, the safer the descent could be for me.

"Fifteen times in as many years," he said. Dieter's tone did not betray any nuance that led me to think that he knew the river was beyond my ability. I agreed to meet them the next morning.

My interest in this trip was instinctive. The company was elite and that alone blinded me to most of the realities of the proposed expedition. The Clavey was revered. Most kayakers aspiring to run the hardest, most difficult rivers require a veteran mentor. I would leapfrog my peers with this one trip. I couldn't resist this chance. In the back of my mind, I also suspected Dieter figured I would bail out, thus providing him with a convenient shuttle. My ego couldn't allow that.

There was an element of exploration for them too. Since ours was to be the first descent after record winter flooding, there was a good chance that many of the drops Dieter and Lee knew would be changed. I hoped that nothing would go wrong. My only consolation was that the poison oak, prevalent along the river shore where I was sure to be portaging, had been scoured clean by the flooding.

With trepidation, I drove down the switchbacks to the Wards Ferry Bridge take-out. To my relief, Dieter and Lee had still not arrived an hour after the appointed meeting time. Perhaps I would not have to follow through on my impulsive acceptance of their offer. I started to drive home and make other plans for the weekend. Mixed emotions filled my head when I saw their car approaching down the canyon road. I turned around.

Dieter and Lee arrived with hangovers masked by coffee and danish. They bounced around as we loaded my boat and jabbered about the upcoming run. They were obviously in their element. Wary of my inexperience, I stayed aloof.

Before we all got into Lee's car and headed toward the put-in, Dieter recommended that I put my car on the uphill side of the road to make it tougher for some malcontent to roll it into the reservoir below. I also caught a glimpse of a bottle of amber liquid stashed in Lee's take-out bag which he had tossed into my car.

As we drove in Lee's vehicle towards the put-in I realized that I could always drop them off and come back for my car. But, by leaving my car at the take-out it became clear to me that they assumed I would actually do the run. Maybe my earlier suspicion was wrong, maybe Dieter and Lee were willing to take me along—a risk they apparently could bear so they could share their adventure with someone else. I might have made the same gesture if I thought the newcomer could run a river I loved.

We found the gate on the road to the upper put-in locked. While searching for a way around the gate, we encountered revelers from a weekend-long high school kegger party having a "hair-of-the-dog" breakfast, whereupon our resolve to find an alternative road to the upper put-in crumbled. We were offered, and gladly accepted, what for us was a pre-lunch beer. Now there was no question: we would not kayak from the top, but would start at the midway bridge the next morning.

**DIETER AND LEE HAMMING IT UP FOR THE CAMERA AT THE SCENE OF A "RESCUE" WE PERFORMED ALONG THE WAY TO THE PUT-IN. SOME 30 MILES FROM TOWN, A YOUNG FAMILY'S PICKUP TRUCK SLIPPED OFF THE ROAD. FUELED BY VODKA TONICS, THE PICKUP WAS HEFTED BACK ON THE ROAD. SHORTLY, PROGRESS TOWARDS OUR TRUE OBJECTIVE: KAYAKING THE CLASS 5+ CLAVEY RIVER IN THE SIERRA NEVADA MOUNTAINS OF CALIFORNIA RESUMED.**

The drive to the midway put-in leads through a rugged wilderness ravaged by the 1996 Tuolumne fire. Winter rains had eroded the road to one lane in places. We crept along precipitous edges of denuded slopes. At our camp on the ridge far above the river, we discussed boating, climbing, skiing, relationships, aliens and the Hale-Bopp comet. Dieter and Lee seemingly indulged in all sports with exuberance. They were obviously old friends. Part of me could identify with them, but some stories they told made me ill-at-ease.

Lubricated by braces of 100-proof Southern Comfort, Lee waxed about childhood behaviors not typically considered mainstream. Dieter coaxed Lee to grander and more sordid exposés of his excesses, to the point where I felt uncomfortable with the psychological lashing Lee was taking and also inflicting on himself. Dieter and Lee seemed immune to comments to each other that would have hurt my feelings. I realized the next day's kayaking would be all the more interesting as I learned more of the character of my companions.

Such talk could scare some less-resolute players away from the game. Yet, I never perceived a direct undercurrent of dissuasion in their tales. I wanted to prove myself worthy of this crowd. No guts, no story, I rationalized.

Also, I had grown to live for the thrill of pushing limits to see what happens at the edge. I had suffered many problems in my personal and recreational life because of this character trait, but found the instinct unwavering regardless of the negative feedback that came my way. Incongruous to some, but perversely logical to me was this "deep play" instinct. I was anxious and unsure about the upcoming river descent, but trusted and was content with the expectation that I could portage the difficult rapids and would emerge generally unscathed. I figured my play would not be so deep as to risk death.

The next morning Dieter led the half-mile boat-drag/walk to the put-in without once looking back to check on our progress. He was in the river, ready to go, by the time I was halfway dressed.

The river started out with a bang. Within 200 yards, Dieter and Lee were scouting the first six-foot plunge through a mini-gorge and I was portaging. They each got thrashed as they ran the slot between sheer rock walls. Lee extricated himself from an upside down pin and Dieter was flipped before being spit into the basal pool. He momentarily flailed at the foamy surface with his paddle before rolling up. They both laughed, exhilarated with the "fun" first drop. I was mildly shocked by their idea of fun and was now even more anxious as I intuitively knew worse would come or they wouldn't have put the energy into getting to this river.

On the two subsequent rapids, both Class 4, I capsized and swam. I was so nervous that I flipped more easily than normal and cringed at the prospect of hitting my head as I swam free of my boat.

"Why did you swim?" Asked Dieter as he tossed me my paddle after my second swim.

"I've got my head together better now," I said.

True or not, I had to get it together, for we all knew we had not even begun to see difficult rapids. I feared they realized they blew it by bringing me along. Or maybe it was the lost perspective that comes with comfort at the extreme level—"hard" for one person can be "impossible" for another. Any thoughts I had of walking out of the Clavey were dispelled when I studied the 1,000-foot high, 45- to 55-degree angle walls of the canyon. I was committed to my semi-rational decision to kayak with Dieter and Lee on their grand annual Clavey run.

I was determined to keep up and not become a burden. When they scouted rapids from their boats, I was forced to run the drops almost immediately. Their scouts lasted only seconds before they spied a line, albeit not always necessarily the easiest line, and plunged down it. At one of these drops, I had to kayak off a 12-foot waterfall at a 45-degree sideways angle to avoid a rock at the base of the falls—a move I had never done before.

When the rapids got harder I employed a simple rule—*they scout from shore, I portage*—which spared them from having to rescue me. After their brief scouts, they bashed and crashed down bottomless, boulder-choked cascades. I scampered as quickly as I could along the shore, boat in tow.

Four harrowing cataracts (sheer-walled gorges) punctuated the innumerable rapids we ran or I walked that day. These cataracts were "must-run" sections because portage with a kayak was impossible without complex rope work and rock climbing hardware. At each of these drops, I could not see the bottom from the top as the rapid was either convex or corkscrewed out of sight.

Dieter and Lee perched on the horizon line-like edge of each cataract, back paddling or holding a rock while they scouted their line. I could not control myself as close to the edge as they did, so I just watched their starting direction, gritted my teeth and, heart in my throat, blindly followed.

Just before I committed to each of the nearly out-of-control, pinball-like descents, my stomach tightened, my bowels grumbled and I prayed a bit. I felt compelled to maintain our pace. They would look back and see that I had safely made it to the basal pool and immediately paddle downstream towards the next horizon line. Typically, whitewater engulfed me and I bounced and plunged downward by feel and chance. Since the portages were nearly impossible, and part of me was willing to accept the uncertainty of what might befall me, I continued to run the drops. I was willing to push my comfort zone and find out what would happen at its edges. After a few more heart wrenching rapids, I, too, exalted when I emerged unscathed. My play had deepened suddenly halfway down this extreme river. I was no longer a passenger, but a player.

DIETER KING ON THE FIRST DROP OF THE LOWER CLAVEY RIVER. THE FLOW WAS ABOUT **700** CUBIC FEET PER SECOND. THIS WAS THE FIRST OF NINE PORTAGES FOR THE AUTHOR IN AS MANY MILES.

THE CLAVEY RIVER CANYON IS REMOTE, POISON OAK INFESTED, AND UNLESS ONE HAS ROCK CLIMBING EQUIPMENT, ALLOWS EGRESS BY RIVER ONLY.

Despite the part of me that enjoyed this "touching the void"-type behavior, I felt alone and occasionally abandoned. Dieter and Lee seemed to be in their own world. I guessed they sensed that I would survive and keep up, so they waited just long enough for confirmation. For them, the run was enjoyable, for me, the experience verged on survival. A pit of fear and tension gnawed in my belly all day, causing me to expend amounts of energy well beyond what was absolutely required.

Occasionally, after a speedy portage, I would sit in my boat in the bottom pool of an unbelievably steep rapid, the top of which was obscured by boulders, and watch Lee and Dieter emerge unscathed. Maniacal grins lit their faces as if they had just cheated death. Addiction to this adrenaline surge had brought them to the Clavey for the fifteenth time.

To my relief, the Tuolumne River canyon came into view, signaling an end to the uncertainty of the Clavey River. Since I was already portaging the last precipitous drop, I kept walking all the way to the main river—I wanted to be safely off of the Clavey. We spent seven hours covering nine miles. By the end, Dieter had not portaged once.

Lee had only walked one-half of one drop and allowed, "Dieter's was the first non-portage descent of the Clavey."

Merely descending this heralded river without incident was my satisfaction.

To reach the car we now had to paddle 12 miles on the Tuolumne River, locally called the "T." I was relieved when we congregated in the relatively placid pool, marking the terminus of the Clavey. We hooted with success. The T would be exponentially easier and less risky than what we had just descended because it carried ten times as much water through a significantly lower gradient and larger river bed.

However, the T's first rapid, Clavey Falls, a blind, Class 4+ rapid proved my relaxation premature. Dieter and Lee paddled directly off of the horizon line and disappeared downstream. The river first poured left over ledges and then funneled sharply right along the base of a 100-foot cliff, directly into a swimming pool-sized crashing wave/hole called Clavey Hole. On my

descent I banked left, plunged down ledges and was engulfed in a maelstrom of aerated whitewater at the base of the falls. I capsized and I rolled up only to became stuck in a surging eddy in a cave-like depression under the cliff.

Five feet from the bow of my boat, the river tore by with the power and intensity of a freight train. I had no option. I paddled as hard as I could into the torrent only

**A TYPICAL CLASS 5 RAPID, SIMILAR TO TUOLUMNE RIVER'S CLAVEY FALLS.**

to have my boat wrenched downstream and my head and body whipped upstream—a classic rookie mistake. I was then immediately sucked, upside down, with a sickening downward acceleration, into Clavey Hole, which had been hidden out of sight just downstream.

I was buried in the crashing wave of its downstream edge and cartwheeled back upstream twice. I gritted my teeth, wondering what I'd do if I had to swim. Then the thrashing stopped. I flushed into quieter water. After rolling upright, I saw Dieter and Lee paddling downstream, nearly out of sight. Neither of them had seen my predicament. I understood now that this was just how it worked at the top end of the whitewater scale. I paddled on.

After two more hours of on-the-fly hole dodging, Wards Ferry Bridge finally appeared and we drifted to the beach at the same time. At the car, Lee dug in his bag and produced a bottle of Wild Turkey. "For a rookie, you did well," he said as he handed me the bottle for a swig. I thanked him and basked in the glow of my survival.

By the merit of surviving a revered river descent with kayaking's elite, I did not join their ranks, but recalibrated my view of kayaking's possibilities and unfortunately let seep in a sense of false forgiveness of Class 5 rivers.

HAVING JUST EXPANDED HIS COMFORT ZONE, THE AUTHOR RESTS ON THE BANK OF THE TUOLUMNE RIVER AFTER HIS DESCENT OF THE CLAVEY RIVER. WITH THIS SUCCESS, HE OPENED DOORS TO A HOST OF OTHER CLASS 5 RIVERS.

**Kenny Llewellyn descends Dry Meadow Creek's second waterfall.**

# California's Dry Meadow Creek

## LIMITS OF ACCEPTABLE RISK

THIS EXPERIENCE OCCURRED IN THE SPRING OF 1998, WHEN I WAS 34 AND AT THE PEAK OF MY IMMERSION IN THE CALIFORNIA WHITEWATER SCENE. HERE, ON DRY MEADOW CREEK, I DID NOT FEEL COMPELLED TO HURL MYSELF BEYOND MY COMFORT ZONE TO SEE WHAT I MIGHT FIND, BUT I DID FEEL A STRONG COMPULSION TO STEP TO THE EDGE WHEN CONFRONTED WITH SAVING ANOTHER PERSON'S LIFE.

Campfire lore held that no one had ever run the seventh or eighth waterfalls of California's Dry Meadow Creek. The seventh ends in a narrow, escape-proof pool. Ten feet further, the eighth waterfall plummets 40 feet onto a whale-like boulder centered in its vertical-walled basal pool. Following this pool, a sheer-sided, funnel-like trough channels the creek directly into an 80-foot long, near-vertical, cascade that T-bones a granite wall. Portage before the seventh waterfall is *de rigueur*.

That April in California's Kern valley was no different from any other year. Hundreds of local, regional and international whitewater, rodeo and slalom kayakers had come to the lower Kern valley with their brightly-colored boats in tow for the annual Kern River Festival. Our group tended towards wilderness river runs, not staged competitions.

"Hey, we're planning to run Dry Meadow today," Kenny Llewellyn said at breakfast. Kenny and I had paddled many rivers in California together over the prior year. "Sam did it the other day and says it is a must-do. Everyone is doing it these days, or at least it seems they want to. I've been itching to do it all week."

In a few short years, rivers that were in the realm of only a few elite were now being attempted by less and less experienced kayakers. It seemed a natural outgrowth of increased promotion and improved equipment. This participation trend is no different than what is observed today with other adventure sports.

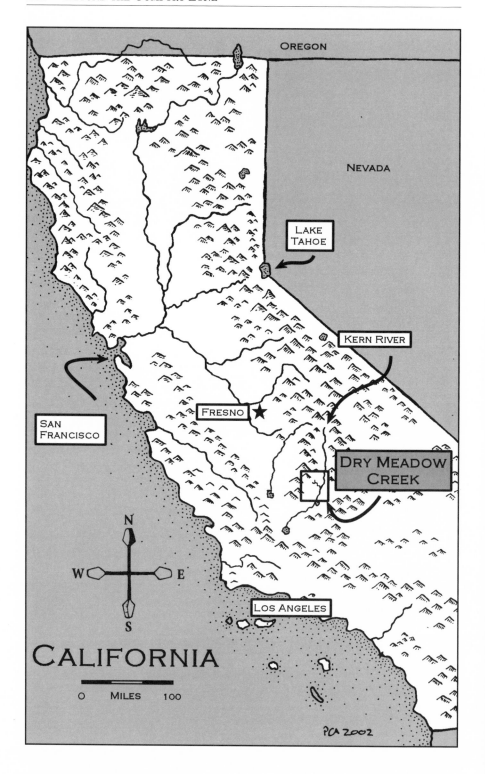

"I've seen the pictures. Isn't it committing?" I had gotten in over my head a few times before on extreme kayak descents and didn't care to voluntarily set myself up for the feeling of dread that overtook me when forced to run a rapid I would normally portage.

"Dude, you can walk around the crux section no problem."

I trusted him.

Kenny had been paddling in the Kern River valley all week with fellow Tahoe locals Mark "Jake" Jacobson, Sam Solomon and Jason Hansford, and a Chilean visitor, Roark Westland—all strong paddlers.

While paddling a Class 5 section of the Kern River earlier that week, Kenny and Jake stopped to portage what they considered an unsafe rapid. The rapid would have required the kayaker to bash down through partially water-covered Volkswagen-sized boulders and up against a dangerously-undercut rock wall onto which all of the river's water piled. Roark looked at the rapid quietly, disregarded their proffered advice and proceeded to get roughed up and nearly pinned against a rock near the bottom as he ran it. With little overt reaction, Roark appeared to take the punishment in stride, seemingly content with the consequences of his choice.

While paddling Brush Creek the next day, elements of Roark's character became more apparent. A Class 5 tributary to the Kern, Brush Creek's long torrents of channelized water are punctuated by blind 15-foot waterfalls. Jake knew the safe lines. On those occasions when the group stopped to scout, despite Jake's leadership, Roark jockeyed into first position to run the rapid. Kenny said the vibe he got was, "get out of my way."

**Brush Creek, *the* warm-up for Dry Meadow Creek.**

They described Roark's paddling style as seemingly bold, competitive and individualistic and perhaps even reckless.

Roark picked the paddlers' minds around the campfire and studied the California whitewater guidebook. He showed distinct interest in sections of rivers that had yet to see complete descents. Roark specifically focused on Dry Meadow Creek as it was only 30 minutes away by car. He wanted to know why it could not be run to its confluence with the Kern.

Other campfire discussions lead to an article written by professional kayaker Corran Addison. Corran, a founder of Riot Kayaks, Ltd., is an unabashed promoter of his industry and holds strong opinions on a wealth of subjects. His bully pulpit had been recently amplified by a second place result in the World Rodeo Kayak Championships. Corran's intellectual and athletic abilities are always on display.

In the article, Corran mentioned that whitewater kayaking needed to evolve to capture broad consumer and commercial appeal—like snowboarding—for it to survive as a sport. He promoted a new breed of kayakers who would bring commercial success and supplant the "radical, bearded, tree-hugging fairies" who had dominated whitewater kayaking since the 1960s. Kenny said Roark's tone and thinly-veiled criticism of Corran after reading this section of the article, might just as well have been spoken: "Who the hell does this guy think he is?" Roark sported a grey beard and had been kayaking nearly as long as Corran had been alive.

Roark shared stories with his new Californian paddling companions. Mostly the stories were of his many first ascents and descents of mountains and rivers in Chile. His sporting accomplishments in Chile were on par with American mountain and river legends Yvon Chouinard and Royal Robbins. Roark showed a polite and self-deprecating manner that, at times, ran counter to what was observed on the river.

One particular story he told about himself to Kenny and Jake that night gave insight into his paddling style. "One day Graham Hopkinson and I were dropped off by helicopter on the Andes divide for the third descent of Nireco Canyon on the Bio Bio. We had done the first and second descents earlier that year and knew it cold. We were to be videoed from the chopper. I got caught in holes, rolled and stuttered my way down a run that I had wired. The pressure of the chopper gave me a nearly-fatal case of stage fright."

As we headed out for Dry Meadow Creek, our group included Kenny,

Jason, Sam, Roark, Chad Parker, three non-kayaking spectators and myself. As I contemplated that day's forthcoming adventure, I thought about how many times I had seen images of Dry Meadow's crux or had heard it described around the campfire. Having recently kayaked some of California's test pieces and having just spent a month kayaking the classic Class 5 rivers of Chile, I couldn't wait to see how this run matched up.

**From left, the author (hidden), Jason Hansford, Kenny Llewellyn and Roark Westland gear-up near the put-in to Dry Meadow Creek.**

We carried or dragged our boats down the mile-long trail, donned our dry tops, helmets, neoprene spray skirts and life vests and commenced kayaking. At times our passage was impeded by brush so thick that I wished for ski goggles while I pulled, grabbed and clawed my way through the thickets. Eventually, the gradient increased and I could see that high water had scoured the riverbed clear of brush. House-sized domes and cliffs of granite capped with ponderosa and Douglas fir lined the creek. Instead of traditional rapids, we encountered a series of rock-bordered pools each followed by twenty- to fifty-foot-long, angled cascades over, along and through water-worn rock ledges, grooves and gullies.

I knew my friend's paddling styles, but not Roark's. With rounded bow and stern, the kayak he paddled was well suited to steep and technically difficult whitewater. He paddled decisively and with little apparent effort, precisely descending the sinuous rapids and cascades precisely along the route he intended. Roark spoke little. He spared us the typical chatter of newcomers to a group. He seemed an able, elder statesman of paddling, as his self-esteem and decisions seemed unaffected by group dynamics.

As we approached the crux, a ridge of granite appeared to dam the river's progress. We exited our boats on river-left and all of us except Sam carried our kayaks along a faint path up across a smooth granite slab for a view downstream. Below, the river plunged out of sight as steeply as an expert ski trail. Its banks consisted of smooth granite walls rising hundreds of feet. The creek bed was made up of eight perched, nearly round, backyard-sized swimming pools each connected by waterfalls ranging from 10 to 80 feet tall. The creek issued a constant roar as it dropped all the way to the Kern River about 1,000 feet below us. An apt name for the creek at this point would be "Swiss Cheese Cascade" or the "Tea Cups." My stomach tightened like I had just walked up to the edge of a cliff.

From our vantage, the whole run, except the eighth and ninth waterfalls, was visible (see photo, next page). Chad, Jason, Kenny, Roark and I each immediately concluded that we would not run it. The steepness of the succession of waterfalls and the overall intensity of the setting left me awestruck.

I didn't even need to look at any of the waterfalls up close. My desire to push my limits had found its limit. Just being there was enough. I would portage on the granite slab. The rest of our group wandered along the shore, looking at the waterfalls and considering if they were going to run them that day. Along the way they all passed the sixth waterfall and its pool—the mandatory take-out—marked by bushes growing on its near bank.

About 100 cubic feet of water per second—a six-person Jacuzzi's worth dumped in one second—poured from pool to pool. From experience,

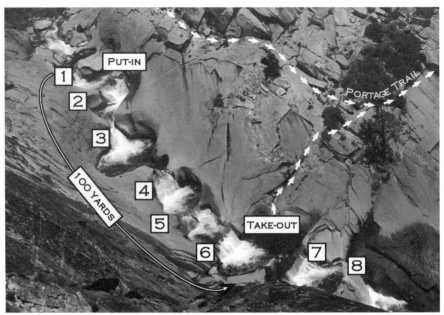

**OVERVIEW OF DRY MEADOW CREEK'S TEA CUPS.**

I knew the momentum of a kayaker in the waterfall's stream would drive the kayak and its pilot momentarily below the surface of each basal pool before porpoising, frequently out of control, back to the surface. Most times a roll recovery was required, a difficult task in this setting, even for seasoned kayakers.

Here on Dry Meadow, I knew failure to roll meant swimming from under one's boat into the churning and aerated waters of the natural equivalent to the ladder-less deep end of a half-filled swimming pool. The only way out was by rope. However, without anchors and ascending equipment, such an extraction would be nearly impossible. Drowning or hypothermia was a real possibility.

My ultimate concerns were the eighth waterfall, which dropped directly on to a rock and the ninth cascade, which slammed directly into the cliff face. Akin to solo rock climbing without a rope, or driving your car recklessly without a seat belt, running this section of Dry Meadow Creek was a no-mistakes proposition in a remote, inaccessible wilderness setting. The consequences of swimming here could easily be fatal.

I positioned myself at the take-out pool's edge with safety rope in hand. Sam, having run these waterfalls before, was game to go again. He positioned his kayak on a narrow rock shelf above the first pool, stretched his muscles, squirmed into his boat, sealed his kayak's cockpit with his watertight, neoprene skirt and mentally prepared himself for the upcoming descent.

Just then, a group of professional kayakers sponsored by the Canadian kayak manufacturer Riot, emerged upstream and moved to scout the waterfalls. Their entourage included Steve Fisher, Ross Henry, Nathan Seeby and, coincidentally, Corran Addison. Professional photographer Jed Weingarten and a spectator, Katie Desrochers, were positioned on the river-right cliff top 500 feet above. They used two-way radios to communicate to their teammates below. Now, nearly fifteen people, ten still cameras and three video cameras were poised as Sam tightened his chinstrap.

Sam launched himself down the waterfalls, plunging, then collecting himself and plunging again, six times. Through the cheers of the spectators, he paddled correctly over to the left bank of the river across the pool above the seventh waterfall, escaping the grasp of the eighth waterfall.

Knowing that no more of our group was to paddle the tea cups today, I moved up to a perch above the third waterfall from where the rest of our group watched. There I saw Riot's world-class kayak-rodeo professionals prepare. The "future of kayaking," as Corran had articulated in his article, unfolded before our eyes as the first kayaker descended, willingly adding complex ballet-like maneuvers to what we considered the ultimate challenge.

As cutting-edge professionals who take risks daily to promote themselves and their sport, their philosophy was simple: If you choose to run this type of difficult whitewater, your margin of safety should be such that you don't count on a safety rope to ensure your successful completion of the run. Most of our recreational group didn't apply the same philosophy, but we weren't going to question the elite as they did their thing.

Their cavalier attitude and the resulting carnival-like atmosphere eroded the serious tenor our group felt. On each descent, the whole crowd watched and moved with the kayakers. There was so much focus on getting video and still

**THE AUTHOR (FOREGROUND) VIDEOS ROSS HENRY'S DESCENT OF THE SECOND WATERFALL.**

**Ross Henry lost his paddle in the third waterfall (top). Here he chases it down the fourth waterfall, paddling with his hands.**

pictures that no safety had been used since Sam's initial run down the falls. Confounding the situation, the two separate groups were now mixed together and communication between them was limited to requests such as "Hey, will you shoot video with our camera while we go down?"

Riot's paddlers performed wave-[cart]wheels, waterfall-[cart]wheels, splats and endos as they danced down the falls and through turbulent pools. Professional kayakers are distinguished from most other kayakers by their unwavering confidence in their ability to recover. Indeed, Ross Henry's paddle became wedged between the shear walls of the third waterfall and was wrenched from his hands. He chose to chase his paddle down the drops. He completed the run using only his bare hands to propel him safely through three more waterfalls and across the current leading towards the terminal seventh/eighth/ninth waterfall combination. A paddler in our group in the same pickle would have been offered another paddle or a rope and would have asked for the same.

"Its psycho. He paddled half the drops without a paddle," Kenny said to Jason from their vantage point. "Why did I even watch these people? They tried all those tricks, screwed it up and it didn't matter. It doesn't have to be made that hard." This observation, combined with the allure of becoming one of the few people to have run Dry Meadow Creek, spurred Kenny and Jason to contemplate runs of their own. It appeared now that despite the consequences of going too far, the actual difficulty of the upper six waterfalls was within their ability.

Jason started to visualize a run. He worried about what would happen if he lost his paddle, dislocated a shoulder, couldn't roll up after a capsize, hit his head and how, under each of these circumstances, he would get to the mandatory take-out. He wanted to do it for photos, pride, curiosity, anxiety and he knew he had the skill. Still, he was very concerned about potential exposure to danger because he felt a feeling of doom on that day. He knew that regardless of how well he paddled, it would be only a matter of time before something beyond his control got him.

Roark voiced his conundrum, "I've come all the way from Chile. I've run things this hard at home. But I have a wife, two young kids and a new house now. I don't

**JASON HANSFORD BLASTS FROM THE CONSTRICTION ON THE THIRD WATERFALL.**

think I'll be running it today." While the Riot kayakers did their runs, he portaged his boat part way to the bottom of the waterfalls.

At the tea cups that day, Jason told Kenny he wanted to do it.

Kenny thought, "If Jason can do it, so can I."

Jason's initial sense was confirmed. He thought, "If Kenny's willing to run it too, then it must be OK."

Kenny's paddling showed his nervousness. He and Jason regrouped in the pools after each of the first three drops. Kenny flipped and rolled up in the turbulent third pool. After this, his tension eased and he continued, giving the audience a thrill on each waterfall. He perched on the rim, aimed his boat and took a few strong strokes before plunging off the lip. On the third waterfall he was completely enveloped in the cascade of water, performing a mystery move—where he disappeared momentarily from sight below the water's surface—before rolling up. Jason showed finesse and control throughout his descent.

In the sixth waterfall's pool, both Jason and Kenny let out hoots of pleasure and relief as they paddled across to the take-out shore. They could count themselves among the few who have descended one of the most intimidating sections of whitewater in the United States. Sam and I joined them for an impromptu celebration.

**KENNY LLEWELLYN, FOURTH WATERFALL.**

KENNY AND JASON CELEBRATE THEIR
RUNS WITH THE AUTHOR (SEATED).

It was time for us to move on and portage the final waterfalls and head to the take-out at the Johnsondale Bridge over the Kern River. But, when we looked up to find Roark, we were surprised to see him preparing at the edge of the first waterfall.

Neither Team Riot nor our group's last two kayakers had a safety person stationed beside the take-out pool. Roark's situation was no different. I did not know Roark's river-safety philosophy, and no one else around me brought up the subject of safety. We moved back up and across the granite slab to be nearer the river. Vanity preempted safety.

Roark's paddling style revealed coincident nervousness and intensity. He surfaced upside down after the first waterfall and attempted two Eskimo rolls before he succeeded on his third try. Spectators yelled "back-paddle" hoping Roark would take time for recovery and avoid running off of the second waterfall out of control. Most kayakers rest after struggling to roll. But, without hesitation, Roark angled his boat correctly to the lip of the next waterfall and paddled off—only to have to roll again in the next pool.

SAFETY TOOK A BACK SEAT TO CAPTURING THE ACTION, INTENSITY AND SCENERY OF DRY MEADOW'S TEA CUPS. THE KAYAKER RESTS ONE POOL ABOVE THE COMMON TAKE-OUT.

Like others before, on the third waterfall he accelerated sharply and was enveloped in the column of water. He surfaced upright and circled once in the pool just below the crowd who called out again asking him to slow down and give them time to move down to the second viewpoint. Roark appeared to not even notice their requests and continued his determined descent in a near trance. It was as if the pools he was running now were to be dispatched as fast as possible.

He plunged down the fourth waterfall without mishap or rest. In the pool below the fifth waterfall Roark capsized and rolled up a third time. Without any hesitation, Roark plunged down the sixth waterfall where, at its base, he stopped for the first time, braced against the rock shore on river-right.

There had been palpable tension during Roark's descent. Now that he was through, the crowd breathed a sigh of relief. I presumed that Roark, like every other boater that day, would paddle across to the distinctive bushy bank of the take-out pool.

As I turned towards the portage trail, I saw Roark pushing off the far shore and paddle forward towards the edge of the seventh waterfall. Others who also saw him proceed remembered Roark either tentatively paddling forward or back-paddling as he slipped irreversibly over the tiered seventh drop. However, all clearly remember him paddling deliberately, as one would above any waterfall's lip, across the eighth waterfall's pool, angling sharply left and disappearing over the horizon.

"He's dead," Corran shouted. He had briefly looked at the 40-foot-high eighth drop, evaluated its feasibility, and concluded it was suicidal.

We moved all-together downstream to look, expecting to see Roark gone, swept to sure death at the base of the 80-foot-tall ninth waterfall. What we saw raised my hopes. A blue-helmeted head floated twenty feet from base of the eighth waterfall, near the far shore. No boat or paddle was visible.

Peering down over the edge of the eighth waterfall for the first time, I saw a four-foot wide gap between the rock and the vertical shore at the left-hand base of the falls. He landed somewhere near, or possibly in, this gap.

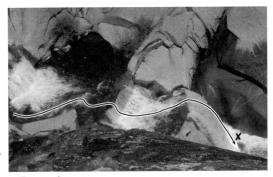

**ROARK'S PATH THE SEVENTH AND EIGHTH WATERFALLS ON CALIFORNIA'S DRY MEADOW CREEK.**

Roark appeared conscious, but wasn't making any swimming motions. He floated on the line between the downstream current and swirling backwater. Luck seemed to be the only thing that kept him from being swept further downstream. The shore leading to Roark was water-slickened, crowned granite that steepened to vertical twenty feet above where it met the river. Roark swirled out of control over sixty feet away. No one could get near the river's edge. The severity of the terrain was such that most would-be rescuers stayed put on flatter ground to avoid becoming victims themselves. Coincidentally, it was the one person who Roark had criticized earlier in the week who thrust himself into the forefront of the rescue attempt.

"Swim to the right," shouted Corran over the melee of shouting people and thundering river. Nathan Seeby signaled Roark to see if he was OK. There was no reciprocal signal. Something was wrong with his arms. This suggested that even if a throw rope were to reach him, he would not be able to grasp it. The consequences of a 40-foot fall (internal injuries, compressed spine, paralysis or concussion) did not escape the crowd on the shore. Furthermore, if Roark were seriously injured in this setting, it was unlikely that he would survive long enough to make it to a hospital. Twelve anxious people scrambled up and down and back and forth along the treacherous bank looking for access.

Corran briefly entertained a running, "Superman-like," jump across the pool. The distance was great, the water swift and the consequences and benefits of this were uncertain at best. His cardinal rule—*never risk your life to save someone else's*—prompted him to stay put.

Nathan moved down to the beached kayaks and retrieved safety throw-ropes. These ropes were strong enough to double as climbing-type ropes if necessary. Nathan threw them up to others who considered using them to string a safety line from a nearby tree, but the distance was too great. They edged carefully towards the accident pool unprotected. None of the throw ropes came close to reaching Roark.

**Path before and after impact. "S" marks site where Roark floated after the accident.**

Corran, recognizing the gravity of the situation, raised his two-way radio. "Katie and Jed, we have a

THE EIGHTH WATERFALL VIEWED FROM THE SOUTH. BY CLIMBING UNROPED ON **5.10** DIFFICULTY ROCK BEHIND ITS CURTAIN OF WATER, CORRAN ADDISON BROKE HIS RULE: *NEVER RISK YOUR OWN LIFE TO SAVE ANOTHER'S.*

serious accident here. I think a helicopter rescue will be needed, stand by for confirmation," he said succinctly, suggesting to me that an accident on a river descent that blended rock climbing and kayaking was one he had encountered before.

Time was running out for Roark, as the water in the river was 40°F snowmelt. Roark needed to be pulled out of the water within minutes if he were to survive, otherwise a helicopter would not be needed, just a land-based body recovery team.

Accessing Roark was a puzzling issue. Crossing the funnel chute below the capture pool seemed impossible. It was too wide to jump. Downstream access was out of the question because of impassable cliffs. Upstream crossing options existed in shallow river sections above where the cliffs constricted flow. This access required a two-mile walk, around cliffs and through bush, followed by a 500-foot rappel descent down a 60-degree gully to reach river level again. Roark would be dead by the time anyone reached going that way.

Everyone except Corran was stumped by the Swiss-cheese geometry of the riverbed. He saw an option that no one else even considered. It would take raw courage and put rescuers at risk, but could make the difference between life and death. Corran instructed Sam to move downriver and set up safety that would keep Corran from being swept down the 80-foot ninth waterfall if his plan failed.

The eighth waterfall, down which Roark had plunged, was 20 feet wide by 40 feet high. Nearly-vertical walls encircled it and its basal pool. At half height, directly behind the curtain of water, there was a weakness. A horizontal, cave-like shelf ended at a treed platform. The problem was that this shelf started just after a seemingly impassable bulge on its side nearest to the rescuers.

The area around the bulge was dark, running wet with water and shrouded in spray and deafening noise from the impact zone 20 feet below. The pounding water of the falls was only six feet out from the wall. I saw Corran creep up to the bulge and delicately test a small hold with his outside foot. Then, arms spread Christ-like, he pressed his body against the bulge, trusted completely the one-foot hold and leaned across far enough to reach into the back of the cave shelf. He hauled himself across the bulge and up into the cave shelf. One mistake or slip and he would have fallen 20 feet onto the whale-rock.

He wormed down and along the shelf and positioned himself above the pool where Roark helplessly bobbed.

"Are you OK?" yelled Corran down to Roark.

"My arms are broken," came the barely audible response.

"What day is it? Where are you? What is your name?" queried Corran, assessing the condition of the victim. What Corran was really probing for was morbidly real. Was it worth additional risk to rescue Roark? Had Corran temporarily forgotten his cardinal rule of rescue?

"Friday, Dry Meadow, Roark," Roark responded, confirming his viability.

"Steve, call Jed and Katie. We need a helicopter rescue as soon as possible," Corran yelled across to Steve Fisher who manned the radio.

"Hello, this is Steve Fisher, we have confirmation that a helicopter is needed. It looks like we can pull him out of the water and try to stabilize his condition."

"OK, Steve," said Jed, "I am an Emergency Medical Technician. I need to know what the injuries are, the age of the victim, and his name, otherwise the authorities may not agree to a chopper."

"Looks like we have a 50-year-old victim, two broken arms, possible internal injuries and soon to be hypothermic," Steve reported.

"OK, assuming you'll get him out of the water, we'll go straight to our car where we have a cell phone and call 911," Jed signed off. It was 1pm.

Jed and Katie departed immediately on a two-mile, trailless hike to their car where they found no cellular signal. They drove to the nearest house and called 911. Katie and Jed had a detailed map of California that allowed them to pinpoint the accident's exact latitude and longitude. Jed had confidence that a helicopter would come as he had seen military helicopters on exercise locally earlier that week.

In this part of California there are various local, state and federal agencies that possibly have resources at their disposal with which to execute a rescue. From what Jed saw on his map, these included: Sequoia National Park, which is north of the accident site by 20 miles; Sequoia National Forest, in which the accident actually occurred; Inyo National Forest; Tulare County; Kern County or the local Kernville search and rescue squad. In an attempt to sort out who should and could help, Jed spent nearly 45 minutes getting cut off, transferred and doubted by various agencies. He had to convince three separate people that the situation required a helicopter. Jed finally was given assurance that a rescue chopper would be sent. He was asked to wait at the phone for confirmation.

An hour later, Jed called back, finding that no helicopter had been dispatched. He advised the 911 operator again of the seriousness of the situation, hoping to expedite a decision. Further delays and rebuffs led to Jed's realization that he had exhausted his ability to influence their decision. Jed no longer wondered *when*, but now *if* a chopper would be dispatched. It seemed incongruous that in the United States, with its advanced social system, resources would not be committed immediately in such an unambiguous situation, described professionally by a trained EMT.

Jed now knew his value would be best utilized by returning to the accident. He left Katie at the take-out bridge to advise others and drove to his camp some 20 miles away. There he collected enough overnight gear for two, returned to the trailhead and started hiking back to the river to assist with what he suspected would be a sub-freezing bivouac.

---

Back at the river, the intensity was unrelenting. The instinct to rescue a fellow human in trouble was nearly irresistible. Perhaps this was why Corran broke, or stretched, his rule. Nathan and I crept down to the bulge and checked out the delicate and risky rock climbing traverse Corran had executed. At the time, I had 10 years rock climbing experience, a few difficult kayak/rock climbing river descents under my belt and could lead rock climbs at a 5.10 level of difficulty. I took one look at what Corran did to move behind the waterfall and was filled with dread.

If I made the move and safely got across, I would be able to assist in saving the injured kayaker. If I slipped while making the move and fell myself, I would become a statistic. My gut tightened, I reached out for the hold with my foot, felt its slope and slipperiness. It didn't feel secure. I felt sick inside. Conflicting on a primal level, I debated what to do for a few long seconds. I pulled my foot back and backed away from the bulge. Self-preservation overcame altruism and impulsiveness.

Corran saw that Nathan and I were trying to join him. He wormed up behind the pounding curtain of water and wedged himself in. He called for us to bring safety ropes. It was obvious he was prepared to assist us across the bulge—risking his life once more. The water was a mere two arms' length in front of us—misting, chilling and intimidating—so loud as to drown any conversation.

Returning to the crux bulge, I looked down again and saw the rock on which Roark must have landed near and the funnel just below. Steeling my nerves, I reached again to the uncertain foothold, clasped Corran's outstretched arm and, in one committing motion, stepped across. I crawled over Corran and slithered down the shelf. The curtain of the waterfall was now just beyond the reach of an outstretched hand. I saw Nathan grit his teeth and repeat my move.

I was amazed that anyone could have made that move unassisted. Not only had Corran just done it, but he came back to act as an unprotected anchor while we made the same desperate move. It was entirely possible that if either Nathan or I slipped mid-move he could have been pulled off trying to hold us.

Three rescuers were now on the treed platform 15 feet above the pool in which Roark was still slowly spinning. He followed our movements with just his eyes. He must have been nearly frozen.

Holding a throw-rope secured to a tree on the platform, Corran jumped 15 feet into the river. He swam over to Roark, attached the rope with a carabiner to Roark's life vest and signaled to us to reel him in. They beached on a flat shelf directly below us.

Corran climbed the rope hand-over-hand, Spiderman-like up the wall. However, the kayak safety rope was only 6 millimeters in diameter, making it nearly impossible for Corran to grip it tightly enough to haul himself up the last feet of the sheer face. He missed grabbing my outstretched hand by inches. Totally committed to his lunge, he fell unimpeded to the flat rock shelf, smacked his knee, deflected off of Roark and splashed into the pool, momentarily stunned by the impact.

The current tugged him toward the funnel and the 80-foot waterfall below. With an obvious adrenaline surge, Corran swam back to the ledge, leaped out, grabbed the rope again and, this time, with Nathan holding my vest, I reached much further down. Corran and I locked forearms and he stopped risking becoming a victim for the third time that day.

We three then hauled Roark up, using friction from the tree to lock off the rope as we lifted. He arrived on our branchy, misty ledge with blue lips and an ashen face. Barely able to speak, he reported numb legs and painful hips. It was obvious that his arms were broken at the elbow from the way they hung limp at his sides. Blood oozed from the wrists of his drytop. He never called out in pain.

Roark looked hypothermic. We had to move. The cooling effect of the mist of the waterfall and the shade from the cliff above compounded our problems. With assistance, Roark walked with us around the edge of the pool to a sunny, flat rock area beside the waterfall's pool outlet where it was much quieter and warmer.

We called across the river to the other kayakers who, by now, had crept down the opposite granite slab to the shore. They threw clothes over. We decided to leave his arms clothed and not dress what we suspected were compound fracture exit points, since the blood flow had seemed to slow. We dressed Roark in another outer layer. In no rush to move him anywhere or do any splinting because we thought that a helicopter was on its way, we lay next to him to try to transfer body heat.

Idle time allowed our minds to contemplate what had happened. Obvious questions came to my mind. "How did you get out of your boat?" I asked, given that both arms were useless.

"I don't remember," Roark responded. Likely he had been momentarily unconscious from the impact. This, combined with the broken arms, made his escape from his boat seem miraculous. Adrenaline and need foster miracles.

Roark's boat, but not paddle, was found a mile downstream later that day. Bow bent up radically and cockpit deformed, the boat's condition confirmed conjecture that Roark's impact on or near the whale-rock forcibly ejected him from his boat. I thought this might explain the damage to his hips.

"I screwed it up. I miscounted the number of drops," Roark remarked unprompted.

"I'm embarrassed at what I've done. I have kids and a new house now," Roark continued. This was more commentary than I'd heard all day from Roark.

"Listen, we have you stabilized, a helicopter has been called, you'll get out of here," entreated Nathan.

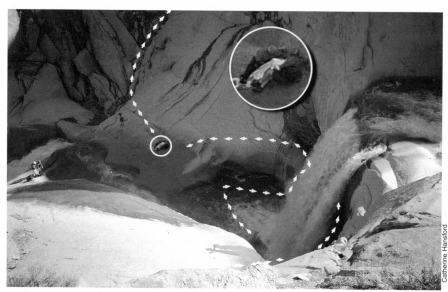

Catherine Hansford

The rescue in progress. At left, Corran discusses evacuation options with Sam and Jason. Within the white circles Nathan, Roark and the author huddle to transfer body heat.

The arrows trace Roark's path from the whale-rock to the eddy line where he swirled before Corran reached him. After traversing behind the falls, Corran jumped in and swam Roark to shore. On land, the arrows indicate the path taken by the rescue party before and after the extraction from the pool.

We settled in, waiting for the helicopter. Roark was sandwiched between Nathan and me.

Kneeling beside us Corran said, "I know Katie and Jed will be able to call out. They have a cell phone in their vehicle at the put-in."

While waiting, the sun sank below the cliff top, bringing cool shade and prompting us to play out options: Wait for a helicopter? Transfer Roark across the river? Wait on that side for the helicopter? Use the assembled manpower on the other side of the river to carry Roark out? The last option seemed to increase our chances, as there was a known trail to the road on that side of the river.

Regardless of the mode of escape, the deteriorating conditions and time passage dictated self-rescue. We broke our heat-transfer huddle. The group across the river cut and tossed over branches for splints.

Our first effort at self-rescue was to try crossing the river. To this end, a raft of two kayaks secured together by two paddles strapped to the tops of the boat was made to transport Roark across the 20-foot wide funnel section above the ninth waterfall. Though good engineering was applied, getting in and out of the raft and the crossing would require a second person to help Roark. Collectively it was agreed that we would not risk anyone else getting hurt.

It was now nearly 3pm; two hours after Jed and Katie had left. Our confidence in helicopter rescue was waning. We agreed that walking out from our side of the river was our only option.

Above and behind us a steep, wet and mossy, but likely climbable gully was incised in the cliff. At about 500 feet tall (half of the Empire State Building) and 60-degrees steep, climbing this gully would require two strong legs and two functioning arms. Above the gully was a forested, rolling plateau that led to a road. This gully was the only weakness in the whole southern river bank. We decided to climb out via this gully and walk to the road ourselves.

Water bottles, clothes and all the extra food available was tossed across the funnel. Ross Henry knew the shortest way to the road. He and Kenny Llewellyn started walking around to the top of the gully to assist with our ascent and hike to the road. The remainder of the group either portaged their kayaks down to the Kern or reversed the morning's journey and walked back to the put-in. They intended to check on the official response.

Sam Solomon, one of those intending to check the status of the helicopter, kayaked downstream to the take-out bridge and went to the nearest house and called 911. He was told that the helicopter had not been sent because 911 had no confirmation of insurance coverage on the injured party. Sam explained Roark's citizenship and the uniqueness of the wilderness setting to this accident. He was put on hold. When the 911 operator returned to the line, Sam said with mounting frustration, "Listen, this guy is bleeding to death on the side of a river. You must send a chopper!" Put on hold again, Sam felt powerless.

"Unless you tell me the exact position, I cannot send anyone in, sir," the 911 operator replied a minute or so later, implying, Sam presumed, that the insurance issue may not actually have been the sticking point.

Sam thought on his feet. "Look, they just carried the guy out, he is right here at my feet. Blood is oozing all over the porch of this house." Sam took a calculated risk and lied. He gave the house's address and hoped his ploy would work.

If the chopper came, he knew he could get in and guide it to the accident spot. He was put on hold again. After a five-minute wait he was told that a California Highway Patrol helicopter would be dispatched. This was at 5pm, four hours after the accident, three hours since Jed and Katie had started requesting assistance. Sam drove back and forth between the house and where he suspected the rescue group would exit the woods. He kept the window open, listening and looking for the chopper.

---

Amazingly, the gully/cliff climb did not faze Roark. We supported him as he walked to its base. I went up first with the rope, securing myself in a belay stance. The lower end of the rope was tied to Roark's waist. Wrapping the rope around my waist, using a body-belay technique, I acted as a human winch. Corran and Nathan clambered behind, pushing, forming footholds and assisting Roark with balance.

The slope Roark climbed was generally smooth, wet and moss-covered rock. Towards the top, trees, soil and shrubs variously helped and hindered our progress. Three times Nathan and Corran fell and tumbled down slope a few yards, a sharp reminder of the risk of this rescue.

During the ascent, Roark was as stoic as I have ever seen a person. Occasionally he would instruct Nathan or Corran how to best support him or to make an artificial foot hold with a hand from below. I was awed by his strength and coordination despite the adverse conditions. He toppled to his side a few times when his feet slipped, but never once cried out in pain. At times his silence was uncomfortable, as he had to be in excruciating pain when his shattered arms cushioned some of his falls. He possessed what seemed to me an unnatural stoicism.

ESCAPE GULLY. FIVE HUNDRED FEET OF UP TO **5.4** DIFFICULTY ROCK CLIMBING. ROARK DID IT WITH SPLINTED ARMS.

The process of ascending the cliff—climb up, set a belay stance, steadily pull Roark up and repeat—continued 15 times over an hour and a half's time before the terrain flattened out. By the time we reached the top of the climb, Ross and Kenny were there. Their ropes provided more security on the final section. Soon we were off the cliff

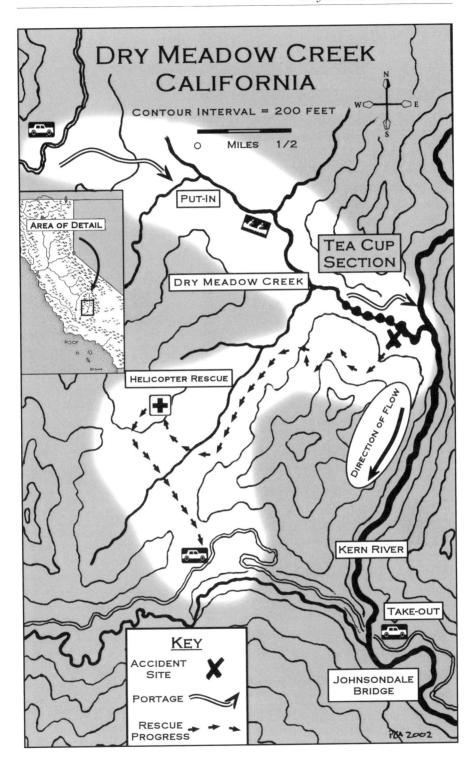

and into heavily vegetated slopes, the accident site now out of sight below. We acted under the assumption that the helicopter would not come. And now, if it did, it was unlikely to see us, let alone land for we were in the forest. Corran and Nathan returned the way Ross and Kenny had come and kayaked down the Kern River to the take-out bridge.

Ross had scouted this river the day before from the direction we were now headed. Therefore he knew a more direct and shorter way to the road than retracing the river upstream to our cars. Ross took the initiative to run ahead through the small ridges and trees and call back to us the most efficient way to get across the terrain. He performed this critical task with dogged determination and poise.

Douglas fir and ponderosa pine formed the canopy while live oak, manzanita, prickly pear cactus, and yucca cactus—also known as bayonet bush—conspired to impede any direct passage through the understory. We hiked directly into the setting sun. Arms splinted with manzanita tree branches that stuck out an extra six inches, Roark now started to shudder in pain each time the splints snagged on a branch.

He walked gingerly, showing, for the first time, the damage in his hips. Dehydration, compounded by blood loss and shock from the actual accident, made him seem spacey. We slaked his thirst with water from the river and fed him all of our energy bars, to little apparent effect.

Finally, after about a mile of hiking through difficult ridge and gully terrain, Ross led us to easier ground along a tributary of Dry Meadow Creek. If we followed a trail up this drainage about a half-mile to a height of land, the road was mostly downhill about a mile from there. None of us carried a watch, but we estimated from the sun that it was about 6pm. The sun set at 7pm this time of year.

Roark's pace slowed. He wanted to sit to rest every 100 yards. It took two of us to help him down and up each time. At best, we were covering a quarter mile an hour. It seemed to me that Roark's condition was deteriorating so fast that we would not make the road that night, or we would have to carry him out. We had no lights, matches or shelter; and, at our elevation, overnight temps would be around freezing. The situation was becoming critical.

When we crested the head of the drainage, we sat down for another rest in a football-field-sized granite slab clearing. A chill had set in the air. Then we heard the faint, but growing chatter of a helicopter. Our spirits soared as it rapidly approached and flew a half mile north and west of our position, towards the river. It circled directly over the accident site.

From our hilltop clearing, we could see the chopper. It was now about 6:45pm. However, with the aurora of the sunset behind us, we were effectively invisible to the helicopter.[1]

Without hesitation, I jumped up and ran back down the trail towards the chopper, vigorously waving a yellow dry-bag above my head. Even when the chopper passed directly overhead, there was no indication that the pilot saw me. The tree cover and darkness snuffed my chances. I could only hope they would spot the group in the clearing. I headed back up the river towards the clearing. While I was still a half a mile away I could see the helicopter had stopped circling and was now randomly getting closer and then further from our clearing. Then, to my amazement, it stopped above our group and hovered. We were spotted!

When I got back to the clearing, the helicopter was just preparing to land. It hovered for minutes, an eternity to us, gauging the landing site. After it finally landed, we learned that this was the pilot's first mission out of the central valley into the Sierra. He said that it was only minutes before darkness prevented a landing.

A paramedic climbed out of the cabin and walked towards Kenny and Ross. Roark sat 20 yards away with me on a log. We expected her to take command of the scene, but she never inquired about Roark's condition or the accident's history, and had to be directed to the splinted man. I relayed to her the accident history as we lifted Roark into the chopper on which he clipped his splint one last time. I saw him flinch.

"He'll be at Fresno University Hospital," the pilot said.

"Thanks," Roark said, looking each of us in the eye.

The helicopter wound up and lifted off. Within minutes we were surrounded by silence.

---

1. Why the chopper did not go to the house location given in desperation by Sam, but right to the latitude and longitude coordinates given hours earlier by Jed is not clear.

Our ordeal was nearly over. Jed turned back from his mission to bring in food and shelter once he spotted the helicopter. Sam and Jason had heard the chopper leave and were waiting for us right where our trail met the road to drive us back to camp.

The next day, Kenny and I hiked back to the scene of the accident to retrieve our kayaks. Another company's professional kayakers were taking their turns dancing down the falls. Photographers and spectators lined the shore recording the "Kodak" courage of the boaters. On the right side we saw a photographer with bare feet who had rappelled down 150 feet of cliff, unclipped from his rope and frictioned down without any protection, all for a better vantage. I cringed.

The last thing we saw before we grabbed our kayaks and headed towards the confluence of Dry Meadow Creek and the Kern River was desperate backwards paddling by not one, but two, kayakers who narrowly avoided plunging, out of control off of the seventh waterfall. It seemed that the allure of this river would continue draw kayakers to its and their edges.

Roark was only 15 hours out of surgery when I stopped off at the Fresno hospital on my trip home the next day. He was under the influence of narcotic pain killers and had full arm casts. Both upper arms were repaired with 10 to 15 screws and one plate each. His right humerus bone severed the tendon that connects the triceps muscle to the elbow. The tendon was stapled back together. Bone fragments were found in his dry top as the fractures protruded beyond his skin. Some chips were missing altogether.

I bid him good luck after determining that he had a flight home. I spoke to Kenny that night and we discussed reasons Roark might have run the final two waterfalls. The reasons for his actions that day may have been as simple as stage fright or as complex as the unidentified force that drives a person to take unknown risks to achieve glory.

---

I met Roark Westland again 18 months after the incident. I found him nearly back to his pre-accident abilities. We kayaked together on two separate Class 5 rivers. From the way he spoke and acted, it appeared to me that his attitude toward risk had not changed appreciably from what I had remembered on Dry Meadow Creek. His behavior appeared to be hard-wired. A discourse or analysis of the psychology of extreme sportsmen like him, however, is best left to more talented and knowledgeable writers.

The kayakers on Dry Meadow Creek that fateful day in April 1998 chose to run what some initially deemed too difficult. Others that day chose to take unprecedented risks when confronted with the plight of a stricken human being. This incident was a stark lesson about instincts overriding reason. Actions spoke louder than words.

The result was simple: one Chilean man was able to fly home to his family and is able to kayak another day.

**AFTER THE SOLIPSISTIC TRANCE OF THE TEA CUP DANCE ALTRUISM PREVAILED.**

The author runs *Curtain Falls* on the *Bald Rock Canyon* section of the Middle Fork Feather River, Northern California.

# Californian and Chilean Omens

*We split up on a dark, sad night, both agreeing it was best*
*TANGLED UP AND BLUE —Bob Dylan*

*And you don't know if it's fear or desire*
*Danger is the drug that takes higher?*
*SO CRUEL —U2, Achtung Baby*

## WEST COAST CHOICES

IN 1996, I WAS SENT TO SAN ANDREAS, CALIFORNIA—60 MILES SOUTHEAST OF SACRAMENTO—WHERE I WAS TO TRY TO BREATHE LIFE INTO AN UNPROFITABLE TALC MINING OPERATION. THE JOB WAS AS CHALLENGING AND REWARDING AS ANY I'VE DONE.

MY RECREATIONAL LIFE WAS ENRICHED BY THIS MOVE. ON ANY GIVEN WEEKEND I COULD CHOOSE TO ROCK CLIMB IN YOSEMITE, SKI AROUND LAKE TAHOE, KAYAK ON INNUMERABLE WORLD-CLASS RIVERS IN THE SIERRA NEVADA OR SURF ON PACIFIC OCEAN WAVES.

IN LATE 1997, I MET A WOMAN. SHE WAS INTELLIGENT, ATTRACTIVE, FROM THE EAST COAST AND THRIVED ON ADVENTURE SPORTS—SEEMINGLY MY FEMALE ALTER-EGO. THIS WAS THE TYPE OF WOMAN FOR WHOM I WAS WILLING TO PUT ALL MY EGGS IN ONE BASKET. I WAS READY FOR A RELATIONSHIP AND HOPEFULLY A FAMILY.

IT SEEMED MY LIFE WAS A PERFECT 10. SOON, HOWEVER, EVENTS UNFOLDED THAT FORCED ME TO MAKE CHOICES THAT WOULD CHANGE THE COURSE OF MY LIFE.

The door to the board room closed. Senior management was assembled. I began my presentation.

"I am here to recommend that your subsidiary in San Andreas be closed and sold," I said. With this statement I sealed my fate. My charmed existence in California would come to an end.

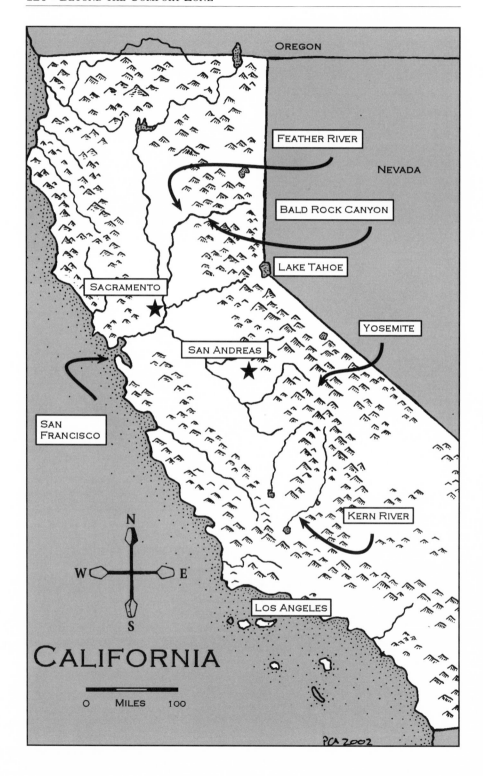

The California operation was peripheral to the company's core operations and profitability was unlikely. It was a distraction to management that needed to be eliminated.

I dreaded the fact that I soon would be one of those business managers who laid off his workers and caused the small town to suffer even more difficult economic times. The plant had operated for 17 years and I had failed to continue its run. The week before I was building, and now I was dismantling.

"How long will it take?" The president asked.

"How much money do you expect it to cost? How much can we get for the plant?" The controller asked.

I hoped to have the plant sold and the mine closed in a year—by June 1998. The plant probably would sell for as much as it would cost to close the mine.

"Bruce, where will we put you after that?" The human resources director asked.

I was torn between working and playing in California and wanting to be closer to my family back East. If the process were to take a year, I would have plenty of time to climb more mountains and run more rivers before I was forced to make any decisions about my future. I shrugged my shoulders in answer to his question.

I left Denver and returned to San Andreas where I planned to gather my six employees and advise them of the decision. I would see that they each received a severance package, help finding other work and proper acknowledgment of their contribution. As I flew, I reflected on my business failure and my failure to find someone with whom to share my California experience.

**THE CREW AT THE TALC MILL WAS LOYAL.**

---

I'll call her Mujer del Rio, Spanish for "River Girl." We met on the Tuolumne River in late summer 1997, two months after the decision to close the plant. As we talked, I sensed a complex and intelligent person whose passion for life matched my own. Mujer del Rio was a lawyer, an intellect and physically attractive. She paddled Class 5 whitewater. She seemed perfect.

On the weekend after we met, instead of kayaking, we drove to Yosemite, at breakneck speed, once nearly crashing on a corner as she pushed to pass slower vehicles, evidence to me that she was as risk-loving as I. All the while we talked a mile-a-minute about life and life's future adventures. She skied, climbed, kayaked, mountaineered and lived life at full speed. We talked of making a great team. But, as it turned out, life was not so simple.

"I hear you are dating the wild one," a friend said one day later that fall. I was surprised by that description of Mujer del Rio. My friend obviously knew aspects of her personality of which I was ignorant. But I didn't pursue the subject. I was blind with passion for this woman who seemingly made my life complete. She drove three hours to visit me. She listened to my stories. We talked about our businesses. She had climbed and kayaked in places I dreamed of going. I hadn't seen any other sides of her personality.

She did warn me that the toughest part of our relationship would be managing her. In the little time I had known her, I saw her be flippant, manipulative and derisive with and about her friends. Even though she assured me her words and actions were in jest, the actual words would have stung me. The maxim about every bit of humor and sarcasm having an element of truth to it kept coming to mind. Maybe I was insecure and paranoid, but I sure felt the vibes. I overlooked these warning signs, for she offered so much more to me than I was getting out of life at the time.

"I'm planning a trip to Chile over Christmas. Do you want to come along?" I asked one day.

"Absolutely, I've wanted to go to Chile forever," she said. I couldn't believe it. Here was the woman of my dreams wanting to make similar dreams real. I thought it couldn't get much better.

"I have always dreamed of taking six-months and just traveling. I want to paddle, climb and adventure all around the world. You know, South America, Nepal, Africa and Europe. I need to see and do those places. Maybe we could do this after I finish closing the mine." I couldn't resist seeing how she would react to my dream.

"We could make a great team. Maybe we could get sponsorship and send back articles and photos to magazines and write a book," she responded. Not only was she game, but she took my idea the next logical step. Our relationship was a dream come true.

We went East that Thanksgiving to visit our families. I noticed Mujer del Rio was short tempered and couldn't discuss her feelings or plans with her mother and brother. At times she was even mean to them. For the first time I sensed something was not right. I wondered if I would become the next loved one to get the same treatment.

We visited my grandparents and mother. When Mujer del Rio did not use the same manners or appreciate the social niceties that I was brought up to value, I started doubting our long-term compatibility. My standards were old fashioned and high, but nonetheless they existed. The reality that there were more layers to a relationship than just adventure mates crept into my consciousness.

Regardless, I stayed committed to her, hoping to follow through on our shared dreams and see what evolved thereafter. Maybe she would change or my sensitivities would harden and standards ease. We both worked overtime in December getting our respective business lives ahead of schedule before our month-long paddling and climbing trip to Chile in January. In my line of business, taking a month off, especially when you were the sole local manager, was unprecedented. I lobbied hard with my boss and he granted the leave, saying I could pick up where I left off when I returned. Mujer del Rio was equally pressed to take a month away from her law practice.

Just before we left, a series of events occurred that defied logic and left me flabbergasted with her behavior. I realized that I had never been in a dysfunctional relationship that provoked me to raise my voice and act out of my normal character. It seemed that just when we were getting really close she would push me away. A Devo song lyric came to mind: "You want it, you got it, you don't want it." More realistically, since it always takes two to tango, the lyric should have been, "Maybe it's her, maybe it's me, or just our blend."

Once we were airborne to Santiago, the angst and stress glossed over. We stepped out into the warm Chilean sun and, within an hour, were paddling. I was in heaven.

CHILE'S SCENERY IS WORLD-CLASS. PICTURED ABOVE IS CERRO ACONCAGUA, 22,831 FEET, THE 30TH HIGHEST PEAK IN THE WORLD.

LARRY BERG DESCENDS THE FIRST 30-
FOOT WATERFALL ON CHILE'S RIO FUI.
CHILE IS FULL OF CLASS 5 CLASSICS,
MOST OF WHICH DON'T REQUIRE CHEAT-
ING DEATH TO GENERATE A THRILL.

My friends in Chile lent us a pickup truck and the trip kicked into second gear. We climbed La Paloma (The Dove), a 16,250-foot peak that looms above the city of Santiago. From its summit, we could see nearby Aconcagua, the highest mountain in the South America, some 60 miles away. We dreamed aloud about climbing that peak on another trip.

Our seemingly idyllic trip devolved after a week. An underlying current of competition surfaced. She accused me of things I swore I never said or did. I became angry when trying to get out of my defensive position. I got called "Party Boy" and "Brucie Boy" in front of others, disparaging terms in my mind, not terms of endearment. I had lost my sense of humor. I started to withdraw. I felt sad.

For the first time in months, my thoughts tended towards life without Mujer del Rio. I thought about my family. I wondered what I would do after my job was finished. Where I would live? Sadly, I had grown so distant from my roots and was so susceptible to just accepting the next option that I didn't have any clear direction on which to base my actions. I always asked myself if my current relationship was strong enough to keep me away from my roots? But, until now, I hadn't acted on either option because work dictated my location.

Most of my friends in California were growing older and were finding rewards outside of extreme sports. Soon the only defining aspects of my life would be my personal relationships and extreme sports. Neither of them seemed to allow me to find someone who would appreciate my broader history.

As our relationship evolved, it became increasingly clear that we had different value sets. However, there was a chemistry to our relationship that kept us in its current. This rushing river of a relationship was a place, like most of the rivers I was running those days, that was both exceptionally rewarding and equally risky.

The ever-tightening vicious circle of our problems came to a head mid-month shortly after I nearly drowned on Chile's Futaleufú River (the Fu), a world-famous whitewater river in Patagonia. Our schedule while in Chile was tight and I didn't want to leave without the *coup de gras*—a one-day descent of the whole 30 miles of the Fu.

Draining the Andean Cordillera, the Fu's turquoise water plunges down a valley whose craggy peaks, lush, forested shores and granite aprons make it look like a mix between Grand Canyon, Teton and Yosemite National Parks. The Futaleufú's Class 5 rapids are some of the most sustained and difficult in the world. The Fu is the "El Capitan" of kayaking.

Despite being fit from two straight weeks of paddling, the first three days of paddling on the Fu had taken its toll on me. A normal day on the Fu entailed about 8 miles of paddling. In our camp, a plan hatched to paddle all 30 miles in a day. I knew such a mission would push me to my limit, but the group's momentum carried me along. Mujer del Rio was paddling separately that day.

GATES OF *INFERNO CANYON*, A 3-MILE LONG CLASS 5 TORRENT ON CHILE'S RIO FUTALEUFÚ.

In the first section, in a five-kilometer Class 5 torrent called *Inferno Canyon*, I capsized. Only after 20 seconds of violent struggle against the rapid's shifting currents was I able to roll up. I took minutes to recover my breath and strength. Imagine the sensation of running 200 yards, where over the first 100 you are allowed to breathe and for the second 100 yards you have to hold your breath.

While recovering I looked up to see another of our group swimming the rapid, flailing to stay on the surface and being chased by would-be rescuers. The swimmer's life vest was emblazoned with human bones. He looked like a floating skeleton. I should have recognized a bad omen.

Further down river our group encountered a rapid called the *Throne Room*, an intimidating rapid where all of the water drove onto a house-sized rock before it split into two 15-foot-high waterfalls. The river funneled from 80 yards to 30 yards wide through the rapid. I estimated the depth of the water at 30 feet as it surrounded the Throne.

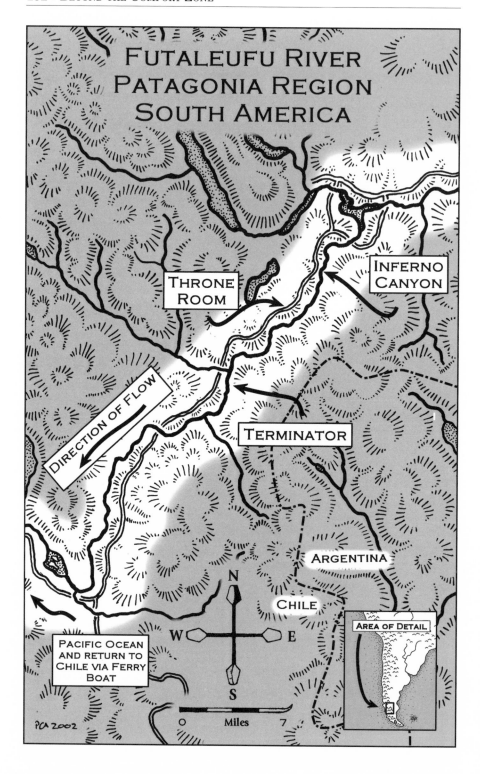

In Throne Room's first wave I was knocked upside down, paddle on the wrong side to roll. By the time I switched it to the other side of my boat, the current had shifted me such that my paddle was again on the wrong side. Seconds passed as I struggled for the right position from which to initiate my roll. The "Throne" rock was approaching. Just as I felt set up for another roll attempt, my torso was compressed. I realized that, despite water's incompressibility (as compared to a gas), I was being driven up onto the Throne rock. The air in my lungs

THE *THRONE ROOM* RAPID ON THE FU-TALEUFÚ RIVER. THE AUTHOR CAPSIZED AND STAYED IN HIS BOAT (CIRCLED), UNABLE TO ROLL FOR 24 SECONDS.

was squeezed out and my lungs started involuntary convulsions. Tucked into a ball, I waited, helpless and frozen in inaction, for the river's power was overwhelming.

Then, just as suddenly as I was squeezed, the pressure dropped. I went over the giant rock and down the falls beyond, buried, upside down in a plunging curtain of water. Like a twig in a stream, I was tumbled and spun underwater for what seemed an eternity before the turbulence subsided and I realized that I was on the surface, upside down. I was 20 seconds in again, and desperate for air, I struggled to roll three times before I finally righted myself. I was at the limit of my endurance and would have swum if I missed my last roll attempt. I paddled over to the shore gasping for breath. I should have been humbled and chastised by the insensitivity of the river and my impulsiveness. This second limit-testing episode should have compelled me to get off the river.

The next few miles of river were relatively placid, engendering complacency. I paddled quietly, deluding myself into thinking I was recovered enough to handle the next Class 5 rapid called *Terminator*. It was a 200-yard-long, Class 5 boulder field studded with pour-overs, keeper holes and car-sized rocks. I had run it the day before and knew the line. As I floated along, I thought if I licked this rapid, I could float easily down the remainder of the river, satisfied that I'd not leave Chile with any regrets.

Starting from river-left, I paddled into the main current to clear a hole below obstructing rocks. In the time it took to make the strokes, it hit home that consecutive days of paddling and two near drownings that day had sapped my strength. I barely had enough strength to clear the hole. Forced to paddle much harder than ever before to keep from getting sucked back into the hole, I just barely escaped downstream. Panting with fatigue, I had covered only 50 yards of this 200-yard monster.

The worst of the rapid was still to come. I fought to stay upright in its crashing waves while maneuvering away from keeper holes—actions that define Class 5. At times I was completely buried beneath the surface and struggled for breath between waves. This river had so much volume and turbulence that even my high-buoyancy kayak would not stay afloat. Ultimately, the river buried me and I found myself capsized. I failed to roll in the turbulence and floated upside down through van-sized rolling waves.

I couldn't hold my breath. I couldn't get my roll—the current was so violent that neither side worked. I was desperate. I was exhausted. Despite the admonition by Fu veterans to Fu rookies about never swimming, my instinct to breathe prevailed. I panicked, released my spray skirt and swam up to the surface. Struggling and kicking to stay above the whitewater and gasping for breath, I was swept down the final waves of the rapid.

I should have swum as hard as possible towards the shore immediately upon surfacing. But I hesitated out of both exhaustion and probably a bit of vanity. Kayakers of my ability shouldn't swim, and if they do, I believed that overt expressions of desperation would erode one's reputation as a tough boater. *Khyber Pass* and *Himalaya* awaited, two Class 4 rapids known for their swimming pool-sized holes and house-sized waves. I was swept inexorably downstream to face the consequences of my impulsiveness.

The total distance to the next pool was half a mile. At 10 miles per hour, it would be three long minutes before I reached calm waters. I submerged for a few seconds in each of the series of entrance waves of *Khyber Pass* despite my life vest's buoyancy. I fought to the surface after each dunking and gasped, becoming more and more oxygen starved. I suddenly realized I might drown. I had never had a life-threatening swim before. I looked for shore and saw it about 40 yards away. I was so tired that swimming across the torrent was near impossible. My heart went to my throat—for my actions had resulted in the ultimate self-subordination of control for fleeting self-gratification. I had taken too much rope for years and now I was going to face the consequences of my privilege.

Unbeknownst to me, my partners immediately set out after me when I swam. Halfway down *Khyber Pass* someone caught up, allowing me to grab the stern of his kayak. I was desperate for air. I tried to climb up on his stern, but my rescuer pushed me back and said just hold the grab loop—for he needed to maneuver around the dangerous holes. I thought I would just ride out the rapids holding on to the buoyant kayak.

Suddenly he yelled, "Let go!"

One of the swimming pool-sized holes loomed. I obeyed and he scrambled to paddle around the hole. My stomach lifted with the sickening drop as I poured over the crest and was driven under the pool-sized hole. I tumbled and spun, head over heels, along the subsurface eddy line. My shoulder hit against a rock on the bottom of the river, driving the last of my air from my lungs. My lungs convulsed, desperate for air. I couldn't stand holding my breath any longer. I couldn't tell which way was up.

I surfaced at what seemed the last possible moment and gulped air. Yet I was still in the thick of *Khyber Pass*. Knowing that I was only half way through my punishment kept me sick with fear. I wondered if I would make it through alive.

Suddenly driven under again, my feeling of dread spiked. I couldn't hold my breath for so long again. This time I stopped fighting back to the surface. I gave into the power of the river. It pulled at my limp limbs. I lost control of my bowels as I gave in to the inevitability of my drowning. My lungs convulsed, but some stronger instinct kept me from inhaling the river. Just before I was going to relent to the final demand of the river, I was driven to the surface by a surge of water. I gasped desperately. Momentarily spared, I struggled to stay on the surface to give me the best chance of surviving what would be another minute of rapids.

My luck didn't hold. I was driven under again. I thought I'd drown now. I squeezed my eyes shut and cried. My fate was being dictated by the river, and I resigned again. Tears welled.

The cycle of surface and submerging repeated itself with each wave. I clung to edges of control over the instinct to breathe. Imperceptibly at first, then clearly, the submergings shortened and my time above surface increased. I began to sense that I had a chance. The rescue kayak reappeared. I grabbed it again. I sensed a calming of the turbulence. I would make it. From the tops of the waves I could see a pool below. My rescuer assured me I was going to be OK.

He dragged me to shore. There I slumped. Never before had I actually stepped over the line between holding on and giving up. I found no pleasure in what I had experienced. I had suffered a consequence I previously had been willing to endure for the thrill of reporting a descent of yet another storied rapid. I needed comfort. I hoped that Mujer del Rio would be there for me when I needed her most.

That night, Mujer del Rio was not sympathetic to my near drowning. In fact, she was angry with me. It appeared to me that the attention I received in camp made her resentful. I tried and struggled to get her to give me the support I was looking for. She finally got my point, but her response rung hollow. I was sad and angry that someone I felt so strongly about could make me feel so bad.

My anger over our loggerheads peaked when I threatened to have her take a bus back to Santiago. She triggered something in me that I didn't like and really feared: I had lost the ability to be light and fun. I felt insecure.

I believed that there was no reason to have to suffer the painful lows of the relationship just to have the passionate highs. The highs were fleeting and the hollow pain that triggered feelings of uncertainty lingered. Yet, like the punishment inflicted by the river as a price of short-lived highs, I had stayed involved with her for too long. As the time for our inevitable separation grew near, we both became pensive. A piece of candy was being taken away. My expectations of a dream life with this woman were dashed. I suspected she too was sad.

We parted reasonably amicably in San Francisco. I was glad to have my own space and to not feel like I was walking on egg shells anymore, but I felt sad and lonely. I found it difficult to explain my insecurity and relationship flip-flop to those who had seen me so happy and expectant before this trip.

Two months passed. We bumped into each other again in April at the Kern River Festival. She was camped nearby. I saw her animated conversations with other kayakers and became jealous. That night, I had a few drinks and so did she. We actually rode to a party together. Verbal parries flew subtly back and forth in the car. The damage started to accumulate. I promised myself when we returned to camp to steer clear, fearing further conflict or a "back to the future" episode wherein we might make up and start the cycle all over again.

Despite my intentions, she followed me to my campsite and crawled in the back of my car.

"You're feeling pretty good about yourself aren't you?" She said. I had just assisted with a harrowing river rescue on Dry Meadow Creek and *was* feeling really good about myself. The rescue team were temporary celebrities. Whatever answer I gave her would make me look bad. It was a no-win situation once again. This was what I must avoid, I reminded myself.

"Look, this isn't working. I don't want to get into explaining how I feel to you," I said. She had made me feel immediately defensive about my instinctive effort to save someone else's life.

"Come on Brucie Boy, explain," she persisted.

I reacted. I grabbed her and dragged her out of the car. This time it was no longer words that flew. We tussled and, for a moment, I thought I might hit her. I gave up when it was clear that I could overpower her physically—my only seeming defense against the psychological torment I felt. She didn't give up though. She jumped on my back, pushed me to the ground and started hitting me. I covered up and took the beating, figuring I deserved it for getting violent. A mutual friend rushed over and broke us up.

It took me hours to calm down. I had just completely lost my self-control. Turning violent towards someone I loved was something I hoped would never happen. My thoughts ranged from jealousy, to frustration over my lack of self-control, to my uncertain future. Now, for sure, she could not be part of my future for I had physically attacked her and surely undermined any basis for trust.

My sense of insecurity and displacement had returned with a vengeance. The next morning, as I left for San Andreas and my work, I couldn't even say good-bye to my friends.

---

Three months before, the day after I had returned from Chile in late January, Judy, the administrative assistant to the engineering firm in whose office my company rented space, said, "Bruce, there is a message from your boss to call him right away."

The plant had been sold over Christmas and I was to work exclusively on the environmental closure of the mine. I was looking forward to it occupying my mind since there was a painful hole in my heart after my break up with Mujer del Rio upon our return to the United States. Work seemed a convenient patch.

"Bruce, seems that we can do your job from Denver. The geologist will do it," my boss, Robert, said.

"What? You said before I left that things would be unchanged when I got back. You approved me taking the month," I retorted, surprised at the turn of events.

"Well, things changed while you were away," he said.

I wondered if it was *because* I was away, not just *while* I was away. I lived a freer life than many of my business associates outside of work. At times I felt they resented my lifestyle and concurrent success at work. This turn of events marked the first time in my career that I had not gotten my way. I wanted to finish this project. I wasn't mentally ready to be unemployed. Now, more than ever, I needed the stability of work.

"Robert, if that is the way it is going to be, I have to invoke our letter agreement we signed a year ago guaranteeing me another job in the company if this one goes away."

I paused and said, "What is that job?"

I put the screws to him more than I would ever have in the past now that my one hope for stability was threatened. I wasn't ready to be on the street and I felt deceived. And, my work ethic was such that once I started a job, I was determined to see it to completion.

He called back an hour later.

"OK, you're back on. Carry on where you left off," he directed.

I had lost my relationship with Mujer del Rio and almost lost my job. The only constant I had left in my life was my recreation. While in Chile I began to realize that to get rewards from kayaking, I had to push the difficulty of the rivers I ran to the point that a mistake was unforgiven. Despite the unraveling of my professional and personal lives, I kept pushing.

I set to task closing the mine. This focus on work allowed my emotional wounds to begin healing. I became knowledgeable in California environmental law related to mine closures, and put together the puzzle of closing the mine.

Knowing that I would complete the mine closure, the company started to plan for my next posting. They offered me two different positions. One, an apparent "Holy Grail" posting in the headquarters office in London, the other as a salesman based in the East, traveling four weeks a month. I declined London, not wanting to start new again and fall prey to the transient lifestyle of a regularly-relocated mining executive. The sales job tempted me because I could live in New England, close to my roots. But, the nearly-constant travel would preclude a life I hoped someday to have. I wanted to act locally and engage in the community. I declined the job at the last possible minute—leaving two strikes against me. Up to this point in my career I had never been forced to subordinate either ambition or lifestyle for the other.

By declining the Eastern sales position, I made any move back East something that I would have to do myself. This action was a direct result of my wanting to finish the mine closure job and the fact that I couldn't give up the adrenaline rewards of kayaking. After paddling 20 of 30 days in Chile, my kayaking skills had improved enough to allow me to attempt a set of rivers in California a notch more difficult than I had been able to a year before. I still desired to flex my risk muscles.

For the mine closure project, I hired local contractors and worked with land owners and regulators. I became influential with these contractors and was respected by local land owners. I started to understand the local politics and regulators. It was heady work and I felt like I was contributing to a community. I liked it.

"Bruce, I'll be retiring in about ten years. I have been looking for someone to take over the engineering firm," Roger Pitto, owner of the local engineering firm who did the planning work on the mine closure, said one day over drinks. He was a respected player in the community. I aspired to his station. With the deals we were cutting on this project, I felt I was moving towards similar respect.

"I'd love to have that be the way," I said.

"We'll work you into our other projects as we wind up the mine closure project," he said.

It was a flattering offer. I could replace the mine closure job with civil engineering job through his firm. If only I had a complete personal life I would have unhesitatingly agreed to join him. I saw his invitation as a way to drag out my inevitable separation from the mining company—a relationship that had proved formative and comforting to me for nearly ten years.

However, in the back of my head and heart, I knew I was setting myself up for unhappiness if I isolated myself in a rural part of California far from my family and the familiar socioeconomic trappings of my upbringing. I still longed to have my northern East Coast leanings satisfied in some way. Ultimately his offer would not work for me, but I hesitated to tell him so because I wanted to keep options open. Every option became somewhat mutually dependent. But, by not choosing one relationship, my hand would be forced.

The mine closure project grew more complex than anyone had anticipated. On the ground in California it was easy to understand why costs were running up and we were behind schedule. In the head office in Denver, my project was seen differently. Senior management knew they wouldn't need my participation after the project progressed a bit further. I saw that time as a few months away. To get there I was consumed by the work. I believed in the project and, despite my goal being to work myself out of a job, I worked as fast and hard as I could.

In the thick of my passion to prove that I could get this job done, one day in June, the head of human resources paid me a visit. He dispassionately terminated my employment. There were no "thank yous," no good-bye party and my boss of three years didn't even deign to call. I went home to the one-room house I rented. My confidence was shattered.

I felt insulted and humiliated. I couldn't look anyone in the eye and couldn't even return to where I had been offered work, for my replacement had moved into my office—right where I would have gone if I was to take Roger up on his offer of partnership.

I had been naively passionate about my job and prospects. Suddenly I was powerless in a community where I had no roots. I was thousands of miles from where I grew up. I needed consolation and I needed to figure out what I was going to do. My world had fallen apart.

My mind moved to the one person I knew understood me, even if she and I had not been the best for each other. I needed legal advice on my separation agreement and my mind immediately went to Mujer del Rio. She returned my call and guardedly offered assistance. I sensed that she was vulnerable too. We each were willing to chance a meeting. The passion we had for each other had not diminished, we had just deliberately avoided each other. A part of me wanted someone to share my feelings with and another part of me sought an attorney I knew who might help me quickly. Her legal advice led to a tenuous restart of our relationship.

Despite my employment dislocation, my confidence started to return as a result of the obvious effort and attention I received from Mujer del Rio. I deliberately dragged my feet getting in touch with my local contacts regarding work options and chose to take advantage of my free time to kayak Sierra Nevada rivers which I had always eyed. I couldn't resist the urge to continue feeding the rat.

While on a midweek kayaking trip to northern California, I found myself focused on my rekindled relationship, but, since it was with the same person who had previously made me so unhappy, I couldn't share my excitement with my paddling mates. I had to hide my re-involvement until I could be sure there would be no repeat of the scorching lows of the relationship. The fact that I felt compelled to hide what I was up to rang a warning bell in my head.

I wrote a candid E-mail to Mujer del Rio spelling out my problems with our relationship. If we were to move forward, there could be no flippant comments, worry about saying the wrong thing, manipulations or picking fights. We needed to give constant mutual support to make our lives work. I put it all on the line in this E-mail missive. She responded in kind, admitting past malfeasances against me and asking for a chance. With this exchange of views, I felt that a huge hurdle had been cleared and a cloud of doubt swept clear of my heart. My confidence surged.

She and I paddled a river together a few days later. We committed to a relationship. In my mind it was a pre-engagement. I should have been thrilled, but felt in my gut there was something still wrong.

Despite my doubts, I resolved to follow through on my verbal commitment to Mujer del Rio. I wanted the security of a family, which, for the first time, she said she would be willing to consider. She continued to practice law and I moved some of my things to her condominium in Sacramento. From there I started the wheels rolling to get back into the work force.

Before I started working again I accepted an invitation to kayak one of California's classic Class 5 stretches of river. This local testpiece was revered by my circle of friends. The Middle Fork Feather River cut an eight-mile-long, 2,000-foot deep, smooth-walled canyon through the granite of the northern Sierra Nevada. This stretch was called *Bald Rock Canyon* and was a notch more difficult than any river I had ever paddled, except maybe the Clavey or the Futaleufú.

The night before I was to leave, Mujer del Rio reverted to one of her irrational moods. My

Dave Good seal launches into Mill Creek, a Class 5 Sierra Nevada river that drains the southern flank of 10,000-foot Mt. Lassen.

Diversions like this temporarily distracted the author from his career and relationship deliberations, but abetted his self-destructive behavior.

heart sunk. She was jealous I had the freedom to take off to paddle, and it seemed that she was angry that I was good enough to do a river that she felt she might never be able to paddle.

At 5am on the morning of my *Bald Rock Canyon* trip, I was sitting at the kitchen table eating a bowl of cereal when she came out of the bedroom. She had a dark flannel sheet over her head and, as I looked up, she looked like the Grim Reaper. I shuddered.

"I'm sorry about last night. I want you to have a good time kayaking today," she said.

I looked at her, not really knowing what I should say. The bubble of hope I had for our relationship had been burst the night before and I couldn't suddenly reinflate my feelings despite her heartfelt intentions.

"OK, thanks," I said. She went back to bed.

I mulled over our relapse to competitiveness and wondered how we could slip back to destructive ground so quickly. My actions were obviously triggering her to act in a way she had so clearly said, only days before, she wanted to cease. It seemed that neither she nor I had been able to change our ways despite our promises.

As I carried my kayak across the condo parking lot to the car, a black cat sat between me and the car. I put this second omen out of my mind as I was determined to leave the disquiet of the condominium and get back to where I had recently come into my own: on the hardest of California's whitewater. I needed validation and I knew I could find it on the river.

Kayaking the *Bald Rock Canyon* section of the Middle Fork Feather was my way to kill two birds with one stone. I could flex my risk muscles and get a day or two away to reflect on the situation with Mujer del Rio.

*Bald Rock Canyon's* setting made me unnaturally reverent as I saw, under blue skies, its crystal clear waters and salt and pepper colored

THE *BALD ROCK CANYON* SECTION OF THE MIDDLE FORK FEATHER RIVER IN NORTHERN CALIFORNIA.

granite. Water poured violently, in frothy cascades from pool to pool, through tight passages and around house-sized boulders. This river made Dry Meadow Creek's first six tea cups look easy. *Bald Rock Canyon* is a smooth-walled, 2,000-foot deep abyss that looks like a giant's skateboard park.

The next day I sallied forth with five other kayakers. One fifth of the way down, our group was perched on the edge of a cascade leading to a pool that drained into treacherous rapid. Each drop up to that point made me feel the same way: nervous and excited about the prospect of a marginally-controlled descent followed by feeling thrilled at having cheated death when I spun around and looked back up at the maze of whitewater and boulders through which I had just descended.

"Watch out for the submerged rock at the base on the right," our leader warned.

I thought, "The other rapids were pretty forgiving and I haven't come close to flipping yet. That rock won't be a problem."

I accelerated down the upper half of the rapid. Engulfed in a wave and blinded momentarily, I flipped just before the base. Remembering the warning about the rock, I instinctively tucked my head to the deck of my kayak. This might have saved my life. I hit the submerged rock head-on, helmet first, driving my head down into my torso. A pulse of pain like I had never felt before shot though my head, neck and left shoulder. The left side of my head went numb, my neck and shoulder felt like they had been stabbed.

I instinctively rolled up and moved to the side of the pool. I sat deathly still. I tried wiggling my toes. They worked. My scalp tingled and my neck was immobilized with pain. I dared not move for fear I would paralyze myself.

We still had four-fifths of the run remaining. The only way out was to continue paddling or wait for a helicopter. After a few minutes resting on shore, the pain receded enough that I felt it OK to slowly move my neck and test the extent of the damage. Nothing changed in the way my hands and feet felt, so I concluded to my concerned mates that I could move without apparently damaging my spinal chord. My only nerve damage appeared to affect my face and scalp and my neck was in constant pain. I realized that my psyche was finally changed by this accident when, despite the fact that some of the more renown rapids including *Atom Bomb* and *Curtain Falls* remained, I wished I was elsewhere. Moments before the accident, running the named rapids was all important, but now, staying alive overrode those sophomoric instincts.

Torrey Carroll

**GRANT KORGAN ON CURTAIN FALLS—*THE* WATERFALL ON THE MIDDLE FORK FEATHER RIVER'S *BALD ROCK CANYON* SECTION.**

Fear for my life dominated my feelings above each drop now. I found myself both physically and psychologically separated from the group who reveled in their descents as I was almost reduced to tears of relief at the bottom of each rapid. I struggled with the reality of my self-imposed desperation.

At lunch I sat very still and, after taking copious antiinflammatories, found my neck and shoulder pain had declined to a manageable level. I relaxed enough to paddle the remaining rapids in the river without further mishap. By the end of the canyon, a dull ache persisted just below my skull and all of my extremities worked just fine. The only physical manifestation of the accident was a tingling all through the left hemisphere of my head, a sinister reminder of just how lucky I had been. I delayed going to a doctor, because the pain had receded to a non-urgent level and my head was filled with thoughts about what I was going to do about my dysfunctional relationship with Mujer del Rio.

As I drove back to the condominium, my mind dwelt on my life's unraveling elements. I was unemployed. I was three time zones from my family and roots. I had barely survived my ascent (or descent) to whitewater kayaking's limits. I knew my relationship with Mujer del Rio was too destructive at times to rationalize enduring them to enjoy the highs. I believed that the Grim Reaper omen pointed to a relationship warning and the black cat blocking me and my kayak's access to my car screamed that I had gone too far with kayaking. With a likely-broken neck and a firm resolve to break off the relationship once and for all, I acted. I would leave my "paradise" in California where I couldn't seem to bring myself to resist the siren call of the rivers in my life.

---

Mujer del Rio was out of town on a business trip when I returned to the condominium from the fated kayaking trip. The next morning, I packed what I needed for an extended trip and put the rest in a storage unit. I returned to the condominium and waited for her to come home. I pulled the rug out from under her before giving our relationship-retry a fair chance. She was devastated. She protested and pleaded until I almost relented. But in the end, she knew that I wasn't going to support her. She pushed back hard enough that the least painful course of action was to split up on that dark, sad night.

The omens then are now clear, I had almost killed myself and knew instinctively that I had to physically remove myself from her and California if I were to avoid the real potential to create chronic pain of a broken home or a crippling injury.

The next day I left for good, both of us ultimately agreeing it was best. I arrived at my father's house in Utah two days later. He sent me for x-rays. They revealed a crack in vertebrae C2, which explained the pain and damage to the facial and scalp nerves in my head. My brother, a doctor, said there is a saying amongst neurologists, "C4, breathe no more," relating to the implications of spinal chord damage to vertebrae two further from the brain than I had damaged. I was lucky.

A week later I reached Vermont, a place literally and figuratively far from California. I got a job at the ski area up the road from my family's chalet and started sorting out my life.

CROSS A 12,000-FOOT PASS WITH A 100-POUND KAYAK AND GEAR ON YOUR BACK. THEN KAYAK 50 MILES OF UNCHARTED CLASS 5 WITH A NEW PARTNER. TOP IT OFF BY ASKING YOUR HIGH SCHOOL SWEETHEART TO COME ALONG AND CARRY A 60-POUND PACK FOR 67 HOT AND DUSTY MILES. WHAT RESULTS IS A TEST OF BOTH RECREATIONAL AND RELATIONSHIP COMFORT ZONES.

# California's Kern River

*Comes a time when you settle down*
—Neil Young

## A RENAISSANCE

IN JUNE 1999, AT AGE 35, NEARLY A YEAR AFTER I HAD LEFT CALIFORNIA, I STARTED A MID-CAREER TRAVELING ADVENTURE. MY FRIEND AND HIGH SCHOOL SWEETHEART, JANNA FORD, WAS WILLING TO JOIN ME ON A KAYAKING EXPEDITION TO CALIFORNIA. MY MOTIVATIONS FOR INVITING HER ALONG WERE AS INNOCENT AS WISHING FOR A COMPANION AND AS LAYERED WITH EXPECTATION AS A RELATIONSHIP TEST. I WAS LOOKING FOR A MATE. JANNA WAS FIT ENOUGH FOR SUCH A TRIP, BUT I WOULD BE TAKING HER OUT OF HER COMFORT ZONE. SHE WAS A NOVICE BACKPACKER AND I WASN'T SURE IF SHE SHARED MY PHILOSOPHY ON ADVENTURE.

In my efforts to minimize pressure before the trip even started, Janna and I had slept an extra hour and were slow leaving Las Vegas. As a result, by the time we reached the trail head, we were three hours late for our meeting with Andy and Anita, our partners for our week-long hiking/ kayaking adventure on the Kern River.

"We were just about to invoke plan B and go on our own. Glad you made it," Andy said. He was understandably perturbed by our late arrival. He had our group's overall interest in mind and pushed to get us back on track.

Our shuttle to the trailhead took until midnight.

"The packers arrive at 5:30am. Have your stuff ready for them because they want to hike when it's cool," Andy instructed as he went to bed. We slept carside, under the flank of the Sierra Nevada, postponing packing for our Kern River expedition till morning.

In their book, *The Best Whitewater in California*, Stanley and Holbeck describe the headwaters of the Kern as "somewhat crazy. . . [having] overwhelming logistics . . . [and] incredible scenery." Snows on the flanks of 14,495-foot Mt. Whitney in the southern Sierra Nevada melt to form

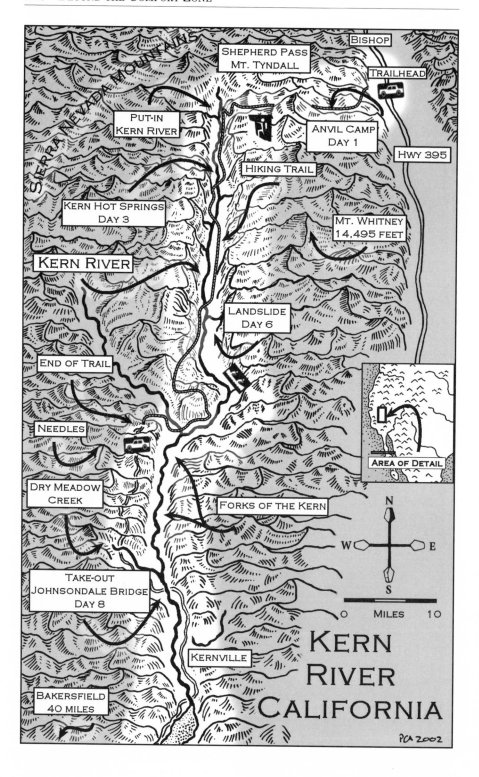

the headwaters of the Kern River, 160 miles from its near-sea-level terminus in California's central valley. Incising a north-south aligned and mile-deep trench along the Kern Canyon Fault, its paddleable whitewater section descends 9,000 vertical feet over 100 miles (90 feet per mile). By comparison, the Colorado River through Grand Canyon descends only 2,000 vertical feet over its 250-mile length (eight feet per mile).

The lowest 60 miles of the Kern River course through flat cotton fields. The middle 60 miles are road accessed, whitewater paradise. The upper, 40-mile-long *Headwaters* section has been descended, on average, once a year since Reg Lake, Royal Robbins, and Doug Tompkins' pioneering first descent in 1981. Its rapids are uncharted, but have been rated Class 5 (the top end of whitewater difficulty) with most parties portaging 12 times around the difficult sections. The near-tree line put-in can be accessed either by hiking 40 miles up from the take-out or by hiking 20 miles over the three-mile-high crest of the Sierra Nevada. We chose the shorter and steeper approach.

This river trip epitomizes expedition kayaking in the Lower 48, something I had aspired to during the two years I lived in California. I felt comfortable with uncharted whitewater at the upper end of the difficulty spectrum. I also loved mountaineering and had climbed a smattering of peaks near where this trip would take us.

Brutal approaches, complex logistics and unknown river character motivated us. My partner for this expedition, Andy Zimet, a Whitefish, Montana, anesthesiologist, is a veteran of numerous first descents in British Columbia and multi-day, expedition-style first river descents and climbing ascents of 6,000 meter peaks in the Himalaya. He knew of the *Headwaters of the Kern* through campfire lore and his intimate knowledge of North American geography. A mutual friend initiated contact and we planned the trip.

Andy never questioned my credentials. I presumed that he may have thought that anyone knowing and desiring to do the *Headwaters of the Kern* was also capable. A few E-mails back and forth and a plan developed. Andy had researched the trip extensively, plotting out each day on 7.5-minute topographic maps, highlighting the highest-gradient sections, arranging for permits and hiring packers.

We would start near Independence, California, hike over the Sierra crest at 12,000-foot Shepherd Pass and access the river at its highest navigable point. We planned for conditions ranging from desert heat to alpine snow. He expected we would kayak 50 miles, after hiking 20 miles to the headwaters, in seven nights and eight days. Our greatest distance from a road would be 30 miles. Our loads would be about 50

**ANITA, ANDY, JANNA AND THE AUTHOR OUTSIDE OF INDEPENDENCE, CALIFORNIA. JUNE 1999.**

pounds of food and camping gear and 50 pounds of kayak and paddling gear each.

Anita Zimmerman, Andy's partner and Janna, my high school sweetheart, would accompany us, carrying backpacks while hiking the river-parallel trail by day, camping with us at night. Both Janna and Anita were novice backcountry travelers and, despite having been told what to expect, were taking a leap of faith by joining Andy and me on this trip. I had confidence in Janna's physical strength. After five days driving cross country, I was looking forward to spending another week with her, having found that we were a super fit philosophically.

### Day 1: Symmes Creek (6,000 feet) to Anvil Camp (10,000 feet)

The low groan of the packer's pickup pulling into the lot invaded my sleep. Peering out of my sleeping bag, I saw the first light of dawn hitting the line of jagged peaks above. Janna looked too and said with some apprehension in her voice, "Is that where we're going?"

"Yeah, the trail goes up there," I said pointing in the general direction of the trail, reluctant to reveal the reality of what we were about to undertake—6,000 vertical feet of hiking—well beyond what was visible—followed by miles of descent to the river. I had sold her this trip as a hike through scenic mountains punctuated by my vision of a moonlight sled ride on top of my kayak from the pass to the river.

"We're not even ready for the packers," Janna groaned.

Anita came over and pitched in as we dumped grocery bags filled with innumerable bags of beans, rice, oatmeal, gorp, salami and gear out of our car and onto a large tarp. She helped us weed out unnecessary items. Andy glanced with skepticism at our heavy foods. I could sense that he wondered: "Who had he chosen to do this trip with?"

"Do you think we need all of this cheese? What about the peanut butter, and the gorp?" Janna asked.

"Leave 'em behind, too heavy," Andy advised.

"You don't need two rolls of this, Janna!" said Anita, bringing to the fore the reality that some creature comforts would have to be left behind. Janna's face fell momentarily, but she remained game.

"What about these ice axes?" I asked Andy.

"I'm not concerned with the snow other than making sure Anita gets over it easily. I don't think we'll need them," Andy replied.

"Please bring your pack over here to be weighed," requested the head packer. With nary a wisp of fat on his 45-year-old frame, John, from Bishop, California, marked down 70 pounds, punched numbers on his calculator and pocketed our $210 dollars (50 cents/pound/mile) and

**WEIGHING IN AT 6AM. FIFTY CENTS PER POUND, PER MILE.**

set off with his partner who carried Andy and Anita's similarly-laden pack on the six-mile, 4,000-foot vertical ascent to our first camp. We followed shortly with the kayaks and remaining gear strapped to pack frames. Nearly nine hours later, we stumbled through a grove of Douglas Fir into Anvil Camp at 10,000 feet.

"Drop us a line when you finish. No one really knows what that river is like, all we hear are third and fourth-hand accounts," the packers said, apparently impressed with our plan to cross the Sierra carrying all of our gear and these huge boats to run an essentially uncharted river.

From our camp, perched two-thirds of the way up the two-mile-tall, eastern flank of the Sierra Nevada, we saw Shepherd Creek cascade down 6,500 feet to the Owens River valley below. Mt. Tyndall (14,018 feet) rose 4,000 feet above, etched against the bright and clear western sky. Between us and the Kern River lay the snowfields of Shepherd Pass (12,000 feet) which we would have to cross using kayak paddles and throw ropes for protection if the need arose. Janna and Anita had never crossed a snowfield or climbed over such large and imposing mountains before. Janna had no idea how dangerous it could be.

Day 2: Anvil Camp (10,000 feet) to Pacific Crest Trail (11,000 feet)

"Janna, I am going to dig a deep hole and bury this cheese and some of the gorp," I said, desperately trying to lighten our staggering loads. Andy was right about our heavy foods. I had to lift Janna's pack to her back and my kayak threatened to topple me over with each halting step.

"Are you sure we'll have enough food?" She asked.

I rationalized, "If we don't drop some weight, we'll never make it." This was going to be a committing trip I realized. I suspected that by the final days we'd be rationing food. But, I knew that without taking a chance, we would never get to do it.

"How does the snow look?" I called out to Andy a few hours later as he started to kick steps across the 45° snowfield. One slip and his 100-pound, shiny plastic kayak would toboggan him 600 feet down the snowfield to the talus moraine at the base of the mini-glacier. He kept his waist belt unhooked.

Once across, he returned for Anita's pack, allowing her to cross her first snowfield without the complication of a heavy pack.

The altitude and our loads slowed our pace to one step for each breath. Janna and I traversed slowly across the snowfield and met them on the plateau above. Here, the view changed abruptly from steep, incised couloirs and valleys to the broad valleys, plateaus and seemingly-endless parade of high peaks of the Kings-Kern-Kaweah Divide.

Only a few hundred feet away was a lake, bound above by a football field-sized snowfield. "Wow, look at that snowfield and cornice right above that lake," I observed excitedly. This was where I envisioned sledding down the pass 2,700 feet over snowfields to the Kern River. But, with only 60% of normal snowfall the previous winter, there were only a few discontinuous patches at the pass and none below. Right here though, only a hundred yards away, was a way to partially fulfill my dream. I could sled down the snow in my kayak, jump off the cornice and skim across the lake. In my blind enthusiasm, I quickly untied my boat from my pack frame and started to gear up.

My idea was greeted with silence.

He was uninterested in this apparently frivolous activity beyond the scope of the trip he had planned. I enjoyed spicing up even difficult trips. But now I had to temper my instinct.

I changed the subject, "Climbing Mt. Tyndall is on my list for later this summer." I was going to return to the Sierra Nevada for some mountaineering later in the summer—part of my training for an upcoming adventure race that fall.

ANDY WILLINGLY SUFFERS LOOSE SCREE, SNOW AND A 100 POUND PACK ON
THE FINAL 500 VERTICAL FEET OF THE EIGHT-MILE, 6,000 FOOT ASCENT FROM
THE EAST SIDE OF THE SIERRA TO THE CREST AT SHEPHERD PASS. FOUR-
TEEN MORE MILES AND 2,500 FEET LOWER, THE KERN RIVER AWAITS.

ASCENDING MT. TYNDALL WITH SHEP-
HERD PASS IN THE BACKGROUND

Andy was studying the map and his watch, intent on keeping us on track. "I had planned to make the river tonight, but getting over the pass took longer than I thought. Now it looks like we might take an extra day to make the whole trip," he said to the group, "We should keep going." Andy and Anita picked up their packs and set off down the trail, leaving us to catch up. What my thought at this time should have been was, "how can we conserve energy and food?"

"Can't we climb Mt. Tyndall now?" asked Janna after Andy and Anita departed. "I want to do it with you. It looks close and easy. If Shepherd's Pass was supposed to be the crux, I can do more." I thought, "Wow." I had just checked my instinct on the sledding and now Janna wanted to do this side hike.

Knowing that a digression from Andy's plan might negatively affect group dynamics, I tried to dissuade her, "Do you realize it's 2,000 vertical. It'll take us two hours up and about that down." In the silence that followed, I looked at Janna and the peak and realized that having such prizes so close were rare.

In a combined motion of courtesy and advice, I ran down the trail, catching Andy and Anita, "Janna and I are going to bag Tyndall. We'll catch you guys on the trail tonight. I'll radio you on the half-hour after 5pm with our whereabouts."

I returned to Janna on the pass, "He would rather we stuck with the plan. But the peak is right there, so let's do it quickly." Spoiling our relationship with Andy and Anita and possibly disrupting the schedule so early would put our goal at risk, but the peak was tantalizingly close. Janna really wanted to do it and I couldn't say no to her.

We climbed for two hours through the car-sized boulders and sharp granite ridges that define Tyndall's northern summit ridge. Moderate risk, physical exertion near one's limit and stupendous views of the local geography reminded me of why I loved mountaineering.

Janna was a natural climber, but the effects of altitude, exertion and exposure manifested themselves in a persistent case of diarrhea. Adding insult to injury, I had left the one roll of toilet paper in my pack below.

"It's normal to suffer the first time you go to altitude," I observed, letting her know she wasn't alone in her experience.

**TYNDALL YIELDED MIXED RESULTS FOR THE AUTHOR.**

On the descent, her gastrointestinal symptoms subsided, but overall physical weakness persisted, forcing her to crawl crab-like over steep and mobile scree, slowing us to a round-trip time of six hours. I had planned on four. I didn't want to jeopardize the trip. It was now 8pm and I knew Andy and Anita were already resting four hours ahead. I was suddenly tense and anxious.

After two hours of hiking in increasing darkness on an unmarked trail that crossed stream channels, wandered amongst grass tussocks and through boulder fields, we were tired, cold and frustrated. "I'll set up the tent here, you dig out some food for dinner," I said sharply over the wind and now biting cold.

Janna had been lagging far behind and my anxiousness was affecting the way I treated her. I saw her biting back tears. All of her efforts were towards keeping up so my truculence threatened our well-being. I hadn't made myself clear how Tyndall might upset the group's balance, and now it was upsetting her's and my balance too. I had a sinking feeling in my stomach that we had bit off more than we could chew. And this was only day two of eight. In 31 hours we had ascended 8,000 vertical feet and walked about 15 miles, carrying staggering loads.

"Andy, do you copy?" I said for the final time, having failed all evening to raise him on our two-way radios. Not only are we slowing our progress, but they had to be worried about us now. We ate peanut butter with our fingers straight out of the jar and suffered a fitful sleep because of the altitude, wind and cold. I was uncertain about the effect of our detour on both the trip and our relationship.

### Day 3: Pacific Crest Trail (11,000 feet) to Junction Meadows (8,000 feet)

We awoke with the first light of dawn, intent on finding Andy and Anita as soon as possible and following through on our commitment to the river trip. I couldn't stand the thought of them wondering about us. I didn't want to look more irresponsible or cause them any more worry than we already had. The way Janna hustled down the trail with me told me she better understood my reaction the day before when we fell so far behind.

After two hours hiking along an intermittent trail, Andy spotted us. They finished their breakfast at the junction of Tyndall Creek and Pacific Crest

**Andy Zimet from the put-in at 9,200 feet above sea level on the Kern River. Proximity of so many large Jeffrey pines increased the threat of strainers.**

Trails and were starting back up the trail to look for us. My heart sunk further, for I thought this was the worst way they could have found us.

"We are here to paddle the river, not climb mountains, Bruce. Let's not have any more deviations from the plan. We have only so much food and time. And the river ahead is an unknown," Andy calmly, but coolly, entreated. They looked worried. It would take time to regain Andy's trust. I felt sheepish again, having been chastised for my impulsiveness. But, already, summiting Tyndall was standing out in my mind as a significant shared experience for Janna and me.

Shortly after lunch we heard the roar of the Kern River from the indistinct, switchbacking trail we followed. The walls of the canyon rose higher overhead as we descended into the heart of the Sierra Nevada Mountains.

We were nearing our maximum distance from civilization. The river ran through forest and appeared to drop precipitously after a couple of miles. Our sense of commitment to each other and our plan solidified.

Our put-in, at 9,200 feet above sea level, was 51 river-miles from our expected take-out point. Andy and I stripped the pack frames from our boats and added gear that had been stuffed into the cockpit of our kayaks to the women' backpacks. I couldn't fit it all into Janna's now bursting-at-the-seams-pack, so I decided to bury the excess. As I dug the hole, I wolfed down handfuls of gorp, knowing that we would definitively now be one day short of rations. I felt as committed as ever.

Anita would, for her first time, be responsible for reading the map and finding the

CLASS 5 EXPEDITION KAYAKING. ANDY ZIMET DESCENDS THE TOE OF A MASSIVE LANDSLIDE

proposed campsites. As backup, Andy and Anita carried two-way radios. The women's adventure would include map orienteering, watching for bears among the giant, 200-foot Jeffrey Pines and enduring 43 more miles of dusty and hot trail. The women staggered off down the trail as we launched our boats.

"It looks like about 500cfs, a good introductory level—not too pushy," Andy said, judging the river's flow as he settled naturally into his laden boat, a glint in his eye. Unknown wilderness kayaking awaited. We had driven 25 and 70 hours, respectively and hiked 21 miles over two and a half days to get to this point. I was psyched to paddle and glad to be done hiking. I was also nervous.

"I've never paddled a boat this heavy before," I said putting my spray skirt on.

I guessed that my boat would feel like a runaway torpedo and I wouldn't be able to make half the eddies I thought I could. I knew to watch carefully for strainers—for trees overhung the river as far as I could see.

Our boats each weighed about 90 pounds and rode deep in the water. Paddling and turning took substantially more effort than I expected. However, greater momentum conversely reduced risk of becoming trapped in a hole.

Andy and I fell naturally into the cadence of mutual support required of difficult and uncharted whitewater. One of us would proceed down river only as far as could be seen from above, where he would eddy out and signal the easiest line to the other. Considering my track record so far on the trip—wanting to sled in my kayak at 12,000 feet and being proven rash and impulsive for following through on Mt. Tyndall—I was relieved that Andy trusted my kayaking enough to let me scout ahead.

At the end of the first day's 400-foot vertical and two-mile-long descent, Andy ran the final 200 yards down steep and technical Class 5 water while I, with throw-bag in hand, took photos. He stopped short of the beginning of the mile-long, 800-foot descent to Junction Meadow. From the portage trail above, this section of river appeared to be continuous Class 5 whitewater coursing over slabs of granite, down sheer cascades and through boulder-choked cateracts. Joining the Kern River here was the Kern-Kaweah River—a tributary of equal size that took a tortuous path through a sinuous canyon and plunged over 100+-foot water falls just prior to the confluence. To our knowledge, neither section had been kayaked before.

**THE AUTHOR PORTAGES THE 800-FOOT-PER-MILE SECTION.**

After a short search, we found Anita and Janna in Junction Meadow. The scenery was magnificent, yet Janna seemed oblivious as she was curled up on her fleece top, eyes closed. "How was the hiking?" I gently asked.

"I fought with that pack all the way. That was only three miles? Forty to go? I'll never make it. That pack must have weighed 100 pounds. It's made for a man's torso. The waist belt pops open all the time and the straps slip off my shoulders," she said. Doubt edged her voice. I was expecting a lot from a novice backpacker. I fixed the waist belt and strategized on how to squeeze more weight into my boat the next morning.

### Day 4:  Junction Meadow (8,000 feet) to Kern Hot Springs (6,900 feet)

The next day's paddle covered six miles of Class 4/5 whitewater with an average gradient of 180 feet per mile. With the addition of the Kern-Kaweah River and then Whitney Creek, we encountered nearly twice the volume of water in the river. We were pushed around more and the rapids felt much faster.

Janna and Anita departed camp before us in an attempt to cover as much distance as possible before the sun cleared the canyon rim, for they didn't have the river in which to conveniently cool off. Their trail paralleled the river, but was rarely in sight.

After kayaking a few miles, I yelled to Andy from an eddy in the midst of a continuous Class 4+ rapid, "I'm going to run the next section down to the corner." My confidence to maneuver my heavy boat in this river had grown.

"Did you scout it?" Andy called back.

"I think it looks OK," I said as I peeled out of the eddy.

I was engulfed immediately in a maelstrom of frothing water, unable to see and desperately trying to stay in control and upright. Seconds later, I glanced off of a boulder and flipped upside down. My head and shoulders careened off rocks as the current relentlessly swept me downstream. My worst fear in kayaking was still getting knocked unconscious while upside down. I cringed, remembering Bald Rock Canyon's neck injury. I tucked my head down to the deck of my boat trying to make a smaller target for the rocks. Skin was torn from my knuckles as I finally forced a roll. Now upright again, but winded and scared, I careened another 30 yards like a pinball and drove my boat to shore. Andy witnessed this reckless carnage and got out of his boat to scout ahead for himself.

Andy signaled back with a X over his head—our sign for "don't run it."

"There's a strainer," he yelled, his policy of never running any section of a river blind just proven correct. Had I continued, I could have been pinned. Taking such risks is never responsible. Nearer to civilization this behavior might have occurred, but here, over 30 miles from help, such risk was not acceptable. The look on Andy's face confirmed the lesson.

We found more Class 5 rapids below and, in our concentration, almost passed Kern Hot Springs, our intended camp.

Anita and Janna had been at camp for over an hour. "We saw a bear today!" Anita proudly reported to Andy. "This morning we saw dry poop, then it got fresher and fresher till finally I saw its leg as it crashed off into the woods—about a mile up the trail from here."

Janna said to me, "I couldn't believe we actually saw a bear. We were so scared after that we sang loudly from then on!"

That afternoon we took turns soaking in the bathtub-sized natural spring at the river's edge. Janna hauled out watercolor paints she had been carrying. Anita and Janna indulged this luxury while Andy and I separately cooked dinners. We shared cocktails of Gatorade and whiskey and talked about things other than our trip.

**Spoils of expedition kayaking. The author soaks in Kern Hot Springs.**

I sensed that, for the first time, group dynamics had stabilized. I felt no awkwardness, despite my previous impulsiveness.

"We made good progress today. Tomorrow we have to go 10 miles to Soda Springs, and the gradient decreases to an average of 60 feet per mile," said Andy, studying the map and marking his calculations in his diary. "It looks like about 11 miles of hiking though. There are many side rivers coming in too."

Anita went over to study the map. "How far to the first stream crossing? One mile? Looks like soggy socks all day again!" She said.

Janna smiled and said, "Let's leave early so we can have another restful afternoon in camp."

That night, we stored our food in bear-tight boxes provided by the forest service. At the close of our second river day, a comforting rhythm had emerged.

Day 5: Kern Hot Springs (6,900 feet) to Soda Springs (6,300 feet)

True to Andy's analysis, the river changed character substantially as soon as we left Kern Hot Springs. The trees gave way to 2000-foot-high canyon walls and city-block-sized meadows encircled the meandering river. Every mile we encountered log jams the size of football fields. We would guess at the narrowest point and drag our boats over. After seven miles of this paddle/guess/portage exercise, the gradient increased and the log jams yielded to smooth-flowing and uninterrupted Class 3 water all the way to Soda Springs. Andy and I had a peaceful, uneventful day and arrived at camp before the women. We reveled in the scale of the canyon, its scenery and the relative ease of our passage.

Worried about our food situation, I borrowed a fishing rod and unsuccessfully tried to augment our food supplies. Sensing that Janna had arrived, I stopped fishing and returned to camp area to find her curled up beside her pack, flushed and exhausted.

"My feet are burning. It was bone dry and sandy, like a beach toward the end, and that pack!" She reported. I jumped to my restoration job—feeding her dinner and naturally carbonated water from the nearby soda spring.

Later she said, "I told Anita that I might cry, but she wouldn't let me. We joked on the trail—she said I 'shot my wad on Mt. Tyndall and was paying for it. No crybabies allowed.' I told her that there weren't many opportunities for more Tyndall's in my life, so I had to seize the moment."

She looked at me and smiled. I felt a flush of emotion. Here was a woman who told me just how she felt. There was no second-guessing involved in our relationship.

Janna recovered, but I remained privately concerned. There was a 14-mile day coming up. And, while the pack was getting lighter, with each day's movement down the canyon, the temperature increased and the forest became dustier and dryer.

### Day 6: Soda Springs (6,300 feet) to Grasshopper Creek (5,840 feet)

"I'll meet you at the edge of the river," I called over to Andy, who was stuffing his tent into the back of his boat. We had seen the women off hours earlier, before the sun cleared the canyon wall. For the first time, I was ready before Andy and was anxious to get on the river.

As I maneuvered my boat over the edge of the 20-foot bank leading to the river, it suddenly pulled me along behind. If I didn't let go right away, I'd tumble down a pine needle-covered granite ledge, over a small cliff and into the river. Instinctively, figuring my hide was more valuable than the contents of my boat, I let the boat go. It bounced once, sliced into the river, scribed a perfect wake and started on without me.

Half of Janna's and my gear and our meager rations were headed down river without me. Lose them and we would have to immediately walk out 30 miles and miss the rest of the river. I was seized with dread and I panicked. I yelled to Andy as I sprinted down stream after the ghost-boat.

Andy sped up his packing and was in the river in seconds, paddling aggressively past me, aiming to overtake my boat. I ran along the shore as fast as the terrain would let me, but lost sight of him and my boat.

I slowed down to a trot and thought dejectedly about how I had screwed things up again. As I contemplated the upcoming epic I would face if the boat and its cargo was lost, I caught up to Andy who stopped adjacent to my boat, which had broached around a midstream rock. I waded out through waist-deep, Class 2 whitewater, aware with each slippery boulder I stepped over that I risked drowning from either foot entrapment or being swept downstream towards unscouted rapids below. I knew from experience in Chile how unforgiving a whitewater swim could be.

ANDY ZIMET, IN A PRACTICED POSTURE, AFTER FREEING THE AUTHOR'S BOAT FROM ENTRAPMENT.

Reaching my boat, I clipped a rope to its stern, saw that everything was still in the boat and carefully waded back across to shore, now using the rope for safety. Pulling hard from as far upstream as the rope would reach, I freed my boat from the rock allowing it to pendulum to Andy. I was relieved, but felt sheepish.

"Every expedition has a runaway boat. This was an easy rescue," he said. I felt better.

The river below this mishap point flattened out to reveal another meadow encircling Kern Lake, a landslide-dammed impoundment. At the outfall of the lake, a massive rockslide from the cliffs 1,000 feet above had dammed up the river and trapped a jumble of logs. Hemming in this mess was a nearly-impenetrable thicket of live oak. As the river reached the landslide dam, it cascaded for a short distance on the surface and then disappeared into jagged rocks and tangled trees—the definition of a sieve.

"It looks easiest on river-right," Andy called out.

"What about that cliff down there?" I said seeing that a portage on river-right would only get us so far before a cliff forced us into the river which, by that point, was visible again.

"We'll have to cross when we get there, otherwise we'll have to go through the oak the whole way," he said. What little river I could see looked like a maelstrom of discontinuous white froth between car-sized angular boulders. How we would cross I knew not. His confident talk quickly reminded me that he was the experienced leader.

Over the next hour, we alternatively bushwhacked on one side of the river or the other, fighting for every foot of progress while dragging our boats. Sometimes we crawled below the scrub oak. Sometimes the bushes were so dense we traversed their crowns. My drytop ripped, my legs were scratched bloody and the heat of the day left me drenched in sweat. It was ugly. Yet, Andy seemed immune to this punishment. I felt as if he had given me a class in expedition portaging.

I thought we had seen the worst of it when we encountered a section of portage that was impassable. Our alternative was to kayak the now, slightly-less-dangerous Class 5+ whitewater—a full notch harder than any we had run yet on the trip.

The river had reappeared from the base of the sieve, and cascaded menacingly through the jagged rocks. To execute this must-kayak section, we opted to sneak along the shore until we were forced to venture into the pounding rapid. We entered the rapid one at a time, the other person standing on shore ostensibly as a possible rescuer, but, in reality, a helpless photographer.

I ferried to the left, above a rocky pour-over, spun my kayak downstream and plunged down a chute on the far side. I barely made the only eddy below, just above the next crux. Andy repeated the crossing and plunged next. This intensity continued for the next hundred yards. Neither of us capsized, but my paddling was jittery and tight. By the end, I was breathing so hard I felt like I had just run a 400-yard race. It was the most thrilling action of the river trip

**JAGGED ROCKS FROM A RECENT LAND-SLIDE BOUND THE RIVER. HERE THE AUTHOR TRADES OFF BUSHWHACKING FOR CLASS 5 WHITEWATER.**

yet. I had bumped up against the line between risk and reward that rewarded a masochistic part of my character.

A mile further down river, Anita and Janna suddenly appeared on the bank and waved us over. "Wow, good thing Anita was paying attention or you guys would have passed right by!" Janna exclaimed.

"We spent more time dragging our boats than boating today," Andy reported.

"You guys will have to do a lot more of that boat-dragging and less drifting to catch up with our tally," Janna said, somewhat cocky and playful.

She seemed to have relished the hike that day. Janna had unloaded our pack and had the food all laid out. I smiled. It seemed Mt. Tyndall's toll had been paid and she had found her humor.

Later that evening, after lounging in the sun, we discussed plans for the next day. "Tomorrow is the 14-mile hike up over Hockett Peak," Andy said. "The trail skirts the mountain on the opposite side of the gorge we'll paddle."

Janna and Anita had known about this for five days now. Janna turned to Anita and said, "No problem, we can do it. Let's hope the water on the first tributary is below waist height!"

"Bruce, the map shows we will hit the falls about three quarters of the way down. There are sections as steep as 120 feet-per-mile in the canyon," Andy said.

"Sounds great, I wonder who'll get to camp first," I said.

"Let's camp at the downstream edge of the meadow, that way we'll have a shorter day the next day," Anita said after studying the map some more.

As we went to sleep that night Janna reassured, "Anita and I will be fine tomorrow."

### Day 7:  Grasshopper Creek (5,840 feet) to Kern Flats (5,000 feet)

The next day we paddled south and east into a trailless section of the Kern Canyon. The women had left camp before sunrise intending to complete their hike before noon.

"No way would anyone run this," I commented on seeing the 35-foot falls. We had been lulled slightly by the relatively easy Class 3 and 4 whitewater and the serenity of the canyon. The falls shocked me back to the reality of this river. At the base of the falls, a truck-sized rock split the river—unavoidable by watercraft. We portaged on river-left using our throw ropes to lower our boats down the cliff and ran two picturesque ledge-type rapids between aquamarine pools to complete the waterfall section. This seemed tame and controlled compared to the gripping portage-fest and scary, blind, Class 5 of the day before.

We rendezvoused with the women mid-afternoon and enjoyed the sun in the grassy meadow of Kern Flat. "I thought this trip would give me more time for daydreaming, but the accomplishments alone are satisfying. Anita and I have it down. You and Andy seem to have a rapport," Janna said.

I felt very comfortable with Janna. I had fallen in love watching her be herself, handle me and relish the challenges of the trip.

Andy Zimet

**PORTAGE REQUIRES USING THROW BAG ROPE TO LOWER BOATS.**

The next night we had to be in Los Angeles to catch Janna's flight. I felt the pressures of our outside lives creeping into the edges of our existence again. Our peaceful pattern of hike/paddle and camp would be soon broken.

"If we leave at sunrise we should be able to make it the 23 miles to Johnsondale Bridge by noon. Any later and Anita and I won't make it back to Montana in time," Andy said before we went to sleep. Outside realities faced them as well.

"I think we can cover about five or six miles per hour on this river," I said, thinking we would have no problem making the distance. The river below was relatively easy for the first nine miles and then Class 4/5 for 14 miles in the *Forks of the Kern* section. I relished the idea of pushing the pace. It would force us to run rapids with minimal scouting.

"Anita, you and Janna will continue on the river trail till the Little Kern River joins, then up 2,000 feet to the car," Andy said referring again to the map. If they got lost after we headed into the 14-mile *Forks* section, it would be a day or so before we could return to help, so Andy reviewed the directions with Anita. The southern exposure on the last 2,000-foot climb had been Anita and Janna's worry all along. "We'll leave before dawn this time and be sure to make that hill before it gets too hot," Anita said.

"We've come this far. We'll make the hill," Janna said.

### Day 8: Kern Flat (5,000 feet) to Johnsondale Bridge (4,000 feet)

The next morning came early. The women left on schedule, following the faint riverside trail. Andy and I covered the first nine miles in just over an hour, nearly doubling our planned pace. We saw the women start up out of the canyon just as we turned south, confident that they would find the car and meet us at the Johnsondale Bridge.

HAMMING IT UP AT THE KERN RANGER STATION IN GOLDEN TROUT WILDERNESS, NOVICE BACKPACKERS, ANITA AND JANNA HIKED **67** MILES OVER EIGHT DAYS, CROSSED A **12,000**-FOOT PASS, FORDED WAIST-DEEP TRIBUTARY CREEKS, SCARED OFF A BEAR AND ENCOUNTERED TRAIL CREWS WHO HAD NOT SEEN WOMEN IN WEEKS.

As we kayaked down the *Forks* section we passed rafting trips just finishing breakfast. They expressed amazement at our journey and the fact that we had already come 10 miles that morning. I reflected back to the mornings six years earlier when it was I who had gotten passed both on El Cap Towers by the party doing the *Nose* in a day and on the Salt by the solo kayaker. The view of the 1,000-foot-high Needles Pinnacles high above the river inspired me. Someday I would get up there to climb.

Trying to keep up with Andy blistered my hands despite it being our fifth day on the river. The scenery and the quality of the rapids allowed me to compartmentalize the discomfort. We ran innumerable rapids with hardly a scout. The freedom was exquisite, yet, I didn't feel like it required having something to lose to be free—for I was well within my comfort zone. I could satisfy my desire to be on the edge by remembering the life-threatening moments of my past. I wondered how long I would wait till those memories weren't fresh enough to keep me from wanting more.

"We are ahead of schedule!" Andy said while we caught our breath above Vortex rapid, a steep agglomeration of boulders through which the river relentlessly poured and plunged. At this crux rapid, the river funneled through a six-foot tall and wide choke point backed up by a recirculating hole. The safer line to kayak was to start center and finish on the right of the hole. I ran it successfully while Andy photographed and held the throwbag. Trading places, Andy seemed to hit the line, but, suddenly abnormally complacent for just an instant, he found himself being drawn back into the hole. A sickening feeling of dread would have overcome me had I been in his shoes. I watched as he paddled furiously to escape the upstream current, but it inevitably drew him into its recirculating maw. My heart rose towards my throat as I saw my leader getting a rodeo ride for what seemed like an eternity. I prepared to throw him a line, but Andy wasn't looking for help just yet. He fought and used every technique I had ever seen, ultimately solving the problem alone and floating clear.

**ANDY ZIMET, VORTEX RAPID, *FORKS OF THE KERN*.**

"I guess I relaxed my guard," he surmised. For the first time all trip, the tables had turned.

When we came to the confluence with Dry Meadow Creek, two miles above our take out, we had time to spare. We scrambled up the steep slabs to the stacked tea cups that define the crux of this famous tributary to the Kern River. I told Andy of the rescue that I took part in here over a year before. We took photos and looked at the awesome drops. Andy willingly indulged in this detour. I smiled to myself.

We reached the Johnsondale Bridge at 11:30am. By noon, the women arrived, windows down, cool drinks in hand. We proudly stood together for a photo, all better friends after our experience, proof that group dynamics can work despite a rough start.

"That hill and the heat wasn't anything compared to the rest of the trail," Janna said, as we loaded boats on the car. I smiled, understanding her feeling of confidence after having achieved a major goal.

As we drove north through the Owens River Valley back to where our car waited at the trailhead, the Sierra Nevada mountains rose progressively higher and higher to our left, culminating at 14,495-foot Mt. Whitney. "If I saw where we were going before, I never would have gotten out of the car," Janna said. She took a sip of water, looked again and said, "But knowing what I know now, I would do it again if I get the chance."

That fall, Andy sent me an E-mail.

"Anita and I are headed to Nepal to do a first descent on the Langu Khola, care to join us?" He queried.

JANNA AND I WERE MARRIED LATER THAT YEAR. OUR CHILDREN'S MIDDLE NAMES ARE KERN AND TYNDALL.

FROM SAGEBRUSH FLATS TO LOFTY PEAKS, THE EAST SIDE OF THE SIERRA NEVADA RANGE RISES OVER 10,000 VERTICAL FEET IN LESS THAN TWO HORIZONTAL MILES. MT. WILLIAMSON, 14,345 FEET AT LEFT.

**AT HOUR 49,** HALF WAY THROUGH A FIVE-DAY ADVENTURE RACE, THE AU-
THOR CONTEMPLATES JUST HOW FAR BEYOND HIS COMFORT ZONE HE CAN GO.

# New Zealand Adventure Racing

*You can't always get what you want,*
*But if you try sometime, you just might find,*
*That you get what you need*
—Rolling Stones

## ANGLE OF REPOSE

IN NOVEMBER 1999, AT AGE 36, I TRAVELED TO NEW ZEALAND'S SOUTH ISLAND TO COMPETE IN AN ELITE ADVENTURE RACE, THE SOUTHERN TRAVERSE. IN THIS MULTI-SPORT RACE, OUR FOUR-PERSON TEAM ATTEMPTED TO LINK, NONSTOP: 25 MILES OF SEA KAYAKING, 184 MILES AND 13,500 VERTICAL FEET OF MOUNTAINBIKING, 15 MILES OF WHITEWATER RAFTING AND 47 MILES AND 10,500 VERTICAL FEET OF WILDERNESS HIKING—ALL THROUGH THREE NATIONAL PARKS. OF THE 50 TEAMS THAT STARTED, ONLY 20 FINISHED. MY PARTICIPATION IN SUCH A DISTANT EVENT COINCIDENTALLY STARTED RIGHT NEAR HOME IN NEW HAMPSHIRE.

The trail down from Huntington Ravine on the east side of New Hampshire's Mt. Washington crossed the Cutler River below the Harvard Hut. In my concentration on dancing from rock to rock over the swift water, I hadn't seen him doing the exact same thing from the other direction. Midstream, nearly face to face, we stopped and grasped arms, instinctively keeping each other from falling in. I recognized him.

"Scott," I said.

"Bruce," he said. We both smiled.

Scott Berk was a rock climbing pioneer I admired. We met while in graduate school at Colorado School of Mines. It had been five years since I had last seen him while bouldering at Morrison, Colorado.

We moved to the river's edge and engaged in a light version of the climbers' reparté of resumé jousting. He had since become a paragliding instructor, been in and out of marriage, worked a few different jobs, traveled around the world and finally landed in Boston. Still climbing hard, he had recently added rigorous aerobic training to his routine.

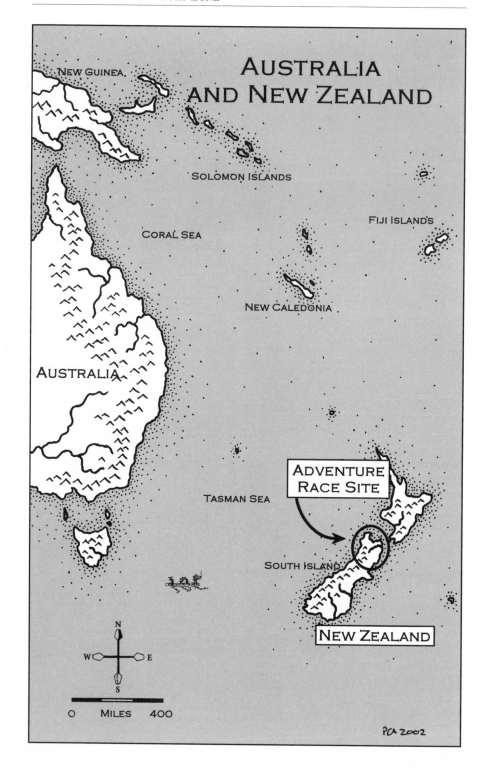

I had faced similar choices that same year. I backed out of relationships in California, ended my mining career and reined in my risk-loving behavior as a Class 5 kayaker. I fled East at almost the same time Scott did.

In the fall, Scott and I conspired in regional adventuring that, while fun, was a notch off of the western-scale adventures to which I was accustomed. By winter, the job I had taken no longer fit. I realized things were out of balance. I had savings on which to live. I was ready to challenge myself physically, but after climbing and kayaking some of the western hemisphere's testpieces and finding my limit of acceptable risk, I needed a new type of challenge.

Scott also sought a greater challenge for himself and had contemplated an adventure race.

"It'll take a strong team, good organization and funding to pull it off," Scott warned. "I looked into the Raid Galouise and the Eco Challenge races. They're so popular that they filled last year. But New Zealand's Southern Traverse isn't filled yet. It's in its tenth year and the organizers profess it to be the 'granddaddy of adventure racing,'" he said.

This race would involve nonstop, consecutive legs of ocean kayaking, mountaineering, rappelling, mountainbiking and whitewater rafting, all sports in which I was reasonably proficient.

"I'd love to do it," I said. I thrived on competition. New Zealand had cachet that appealed to my vanity.

Being successful wouldn't be easy. Mixing team competition with normally solitary or single-partner sports was something I had not tried. My choice on an otherwise free day would be to fill it up with as many different sports as I could. When I lived in Colorado, I could ski, rock climb and run Class 5 whitewater all in the same day. An adventure race seemed a logical next step—an ultimate test of my interpersonal, organizational and athletic skills. I had been planning a 'round-the-world kayaking and mountaineering trip and found this proposed adventure race in New Zealand a convenient vehicle through which to justify my plans.

"Who's on the team?" I asked.

"I am pushing for my brother. Maybe you and your brother could round out the team? I think…"

Before he could finish I drifted off imagining the simplicity of a brothers' team. I had heard that successful adventure racing teams intuitively understood each other's talents, personalities and thresholds. I knew Scott and had once met his brother, a ten-year veteran Outward Bound instructor. My brother and I shared a decades-long athletic history of adventuring and he had spent two seasons in New Zealand. If only the actual adventure race experience had been so idyllic.

U.S. BASED SUPPORT CREW FOR TEAM NO-
MAD, FROM LEFT TO RIGHT, STEVE GE-
NEREAUX, LORI DUPAUL, STEVE "PUT"
PUTNAM, SCOTT BERK, PETER GENEREAUX,
THE AUTHOR, BRENDA BERG, GERRY BERK
AND DIANE BERK.

NOT PICTURED ARE THE KIWI MEMBERS
OF OUR SUPPORT CREW, BRYAN REDDISH
AND SIMON MIDDLEMASS.

While neither of our brothers could free themselves from other obligations for long enough to compete as athletes, they assisted the team in various ways. Filling the team's athlete roster were Steve Putnam, aka "Put", and Lori DuPaul. Steve Putnam was a college friend of mine. Put also was a national-caliber skier, kayaker, windsurfer and mountainbiker, whose industry contacts were critical to our fund-raising and equipment needs. Put's only weakness was an admitted fear of heights, which could limit him, and by extension the team, during the mandatory rappel.

Lori, who lived in Salt Lake City, brought to the team her exceptional mountain running and marathon experience (she ran a 2:50 personal best that year). She thrived on fast-paced athletic competition. Lori joined the team a month before the race, forcing us to take on faith that her athletic history was sufficient enough to not only carry her through the foot legs, but also the biking and kayak legs of the race.

Brenda Berg, a logistics expert and rock climber from South Carolina shared co-chief of the support crew responsibilities with my brother, Steve, who would also serve as team doctor. The rest of the support crew was comprised of Scott's parents, Jerry and Dianne Berk, and my dad, Peter. I was glad to have my brother and father share what I suspected would be a once-in-a-lifetime experience. They knew in advance the reality of life as a support crew member: Long distance driving and long periods of inactivity punctuated by action when the athletes came through the transition zone wanting food, gear and solace. Theirs could be a thankless job.

The team gained momentum and expectations rose as we prepped through the summer and fall. Organizing our team forced Scott (our self-appointed captain) to apply skills beyond his normal repertoire. His success manifested itself in a complete team of athletes, a support crew, funding for half the $12,000 budget, daily monitoring of his and the team's training routines, creation of a website, two team training rendezvous and various corporate sponsors.

Team Nomad became our name, derived from Scott's recent nomadic lifestyle. Our literature and promotional mottos read: *Beyond the Triathlon*; *Grunt, Grind and Grovel*; and *Sleep Optional*. Equipment and direct financial sponsors responded favorably to Put's prospectus and other team member's solicitations. By race time, we were outfitted with new mountain bikes, special adventure racing backpacks, medical equipment, rappeling gear, Gore-Tex outwear, nutritional supplements and a nearly infinite supply of batteries for our new headlamps.

THE TEAM TRAINED TOGETHER THREE TIMES BEFORE THE RACE—IN HOOD RIVER, OREGON, SOUTH RYEGATE, VERMONT, AND MOAB, UTAH. PICTURED OUTSIDE MOAB FROM LEFT TO RIGHT ARE THE AUTHOR, KATY RYAN (SHE TRIED OUT FOR THE TEAM), LORI DUPAUL AND SCOTT BERK. THESE TRAINING SESSIONS REVEALED MUCH ABOUT OUR RELATIVE ABILITIES AND EQUIPMENT NEEDS.

Brenda handled the administrative details. I traveled alternatively with Scott and Put from Boston to San Francisco and back through Salt Lake and Denver, raising money peddling T-shirts and baseball caps at fund-raiser slide shows. We compiled an E-mail supporter list 200 strong and generated hits on our website that peaked at 30,000 during the race week. All told, we were admirably organized from an administrative standpoint.

A successful team, however, takes more than good organization. I was concerned about areas of weakness I perceived in our team. Scott became our leader, a role he found himself in by default when his desire to be an athlete out on the course required a team with the same goal.

Put couldn't get over his fear of heights and there was talk of him having to walk around the rappelling section of the course—resulting in the team suffering penalty or possible disqualification.

We all were supposed to keep training logs for posting to our team website. Maybe it was technical difficulties or time constraints, but my teammates infrequently posted their workouts. This added to my concern that we might end up at different levels of preparedness come race time.

Other issues arose as well, including financing problems for one team member, which Scott ended up covering. Resentment incubated.

Our last group training exercise was supposed to have been a 36-hour straight dry-run through the Utah desert. We lasted 12 hours before equipment, fatigue and disorganization doomed us. Each of them had full-time jobs and could not devote as much time to training as I thought necessary.

While the preparations were fun and fulfilling, our strategy resulted, unfortunately, in a lack of real focus on our weaknesses. We just plodded along on our own agendas naively hoping they would translate into a team effort later on. To top off our travails, Scott developed a cold two weeks before the race that hampered his final training.

SUNRISE AT **39,000** FEET OVER THE SOUTH PACIFIC—NOVEMBER **1999.**

Two weeks before the race I flew to New Zealand. It was November 1999. Fit as I could be, having trained about six hours a day on rivers and mountains from coast to coast over the summer and fall, I was determined to perform at my limit regardless of my teammate's abilities. If my high level of fitness matched the fiendish reputation of the Southern Traverse, then I would return home satisfied. Given the complications and weaknesses of my teammates, however, I should have warily girded myself for disappointment. Optimistic by nature, I carried on.

The first thing that I noticed upon arrival in New Zealand were the nearly continuous and rugged mountains that rose directly from the turquoise South Pacific Ocean. The mountains looked like a cross between the Pacific Northwest of the United States, California's Marin Headlands and the Santa Monica Mountains west of Los Angeles. It looked like a great setting for adventure.

While reconnoitering the areas, I set a opportunity-maximizing schedule for myself, linking mountain bike rides and speed hikes/runs across local mountain ranges, followed by three days whitewater kayaking further south. I had dreamed of kayaking New Zealand's classic rivers and, despite having my first priority being the adventure race, I was determined to make the most of my time and expense. A lifetime of athletics had prepared me for the physical challenges of this Southern Traverse, so I didn't worry if I shirked my training responsibilities for a few days to play out some of my dreams.

During my reconnaissance, every friendly Kiwi I met confirmed the Southern Traverse's "full on" reputation. I E-mailed reports to our team's friends and supporters:

I felt presumptive doing this because, as usual, I was pushing the envelope by raising a high bar of success in an event in which we were all rookies. Falling prey to my normal "no guts, no story" mode, I wired each day's account.

> *Treeline is around 1,000 meters in elevation -- maybe a bit higher. The trails are stream courses and really rocky under the up to a third of a meter of water that run on them during rain. The ridge hike between peaks was on roots and in huge deciduous trees. Some swampy areas. My boots were wet from the get-go. Walking through water up to my shins and stream crossings up to my waist was the norm. There were places where the ferns were double overhead! Going off trail would be nearly impossible without serious misery factor. The slopes are very steep and switchbacks nonexistent. Trails are well marked and there are poles above treeline for finding your way in the pea soup clouds. All in all I did 15 km of hiking, 1,000 meters vertical in 4.5 hours. This included some running on the easier parts.*

Scott, Put, Lori and Brenda arrived a week into my solo reconnaissance and I switched into pre-race mode. We practiced sea kayaking, hiked casually through where we suspected the race would traverse, checked our mountain bikes out and familiarized ourselves with the regional geography. While investigating a possible dense-forest bushwhack, Scott, Put and I got into a long debate over course plotting—an example I thought of an emerging undercurrent of power struggle.

We discussed our team's philosophy and agreed that our objective was to try to finish the whole course together. If one of us dropped out, the team would continue on with a reduced squad—a key difference from other teams' objectives—and finish together or not at all. In the case we might take longer than the maximum time allowed by the race organizers, we agreed to accept diversion to an abbreviated course, thus enabling some type of finish. Some measure of success was all that we cared for.

Regardless of the fall-back positions the race organizers made available, I knew, like before on El Capitan, my success would be closely tied to my teammates' abilities. The rules of the race were: If one person got hurt or the team failed to keep under the race organizer's preestablished maximum time for each leg, the team went "unranked"— meaning it was allowed to continue on course to the finish, but received no official result. If two members dropped out, the team was disqualified and pulled from the course.

LOCAL KIWIS BRYAN REDDISH, RICH-
ARD DUNN, DALE MCDONALD, SIMON
MIDDLEMASS AND THE "DEFECTIVE,"
LYNDA RETTERMYER, SELFLESSLY
HELPED OUR TEAM.

PICTURED ABOVE, BRYAN AND HIS DOG
PORSCHE. PORSCHE WAS SO EXCITED
ABOUT THE RACE THAT HE NEEDED A
DUCT TAPE BLIND TO CALM HIM WHILE
HE RODE BETWEEN CHECKPOINTS.

As the remaining United States-based support crew trickled in, they joined Brenda in clearing final logistical and administrative race requirements. Medical forms were submitted, competency in the various sports demonstrated, media data completed, team photos taken and finally, spare parts for our mountainbikes collected. The final pre-race hurdle was cleared in the supermarket, where a van-load of food for 11 people for five days and nights was procured.

Two-hundred-fifty competitors assembled at the race briefing. Politicians spoke, media and teams were introduced and race organizers and favored athletes identified. Competitors sized each other up and ogled the pre-race favorites. Map and course description packets were distributed. Questions were fielded by the race organizers. The hype was palpable.

Just being at the briefing validated many aspects of the efforts I had put in over the previous six months. But this heady, self-congratulatory moment was short lived as soon as we started to study the course. It appeared to me that the race would live up to its reputation. The course looked relentless. We had no way to gauge the actual difficulty, but on paper it looked tough. I continued to hope that the fitness of my teammates and that our support organization was robust enough to meet our goal—compete in the race to finish. I remained confident in my ability to complete the course.

A more pervasive challenge than the ephemeral physical discomfort of the training and up coming race, was my struggle to be a constructive follower. My history of business and social leadership and personality typically brought my instinct to be leader, or captain, to the surface in situations like this. Team Nomad's stateside training rendezvous had occurred during weekends, the brevity of which allowed me to hold my leadership instincts in check. Now restricted to hotel rooms and one van, our 24-hours-a-day proximity and the uncertainty of our team's abilities compounded my difficulties. An example of my challenge reared its head after I saw the course description.

**TYPICAL OPPORTUNISTIC TRAINING BEFORE THE RACE. THE AUTHOR ON NEW ZEALAND'S CLASS 5 STYX RIVER**

I noted that the second mountain bike leg passed through the Golden Downs forest, a maze of new logging roads that were not marked on our maps. I couldn't resist pushing Scott to allow my brother and Simon (a local Kiwi support crew member) to preview this section via car. Knowing how to navigate through this section before we got there would make our passage faster and less frustrating. Getting lost and having to backtrack could be our downfall.

My inability to be a good follower manifested itself in other ways too. At times I rejected Scott's lead by being passive-aggressive, a destructive trait I sometimes demonstrate when I don't get my way. Other times I was illogically contrarian and impatient before remembering that such selfish behavior was not going to help anything. I should have remembered a lesson explained by my friend, John Hill, years before: *"You know you are an adult when you realize that you can't change someone else."*

My overall objective was to help the team meet its goal, but I wasn't necessarily carrying it out in the right way. I tried to check my leadership instincts, for I couldn't change so many people. The only way to change the situation would be to get a new team, a strategy I had observed in corporate America that brought mixed results. Culture is the people. It was too late to change anything with our team and, in reality, I should have considered myself lucky to be in New Zealand with a team at all.

While the Golden Downs mountain bike leg was scouted, the rest of the team and support crew drove to the sea kayak start, some 60 miles away. We used the time to study the course maps and discuss food and gear logistics. Each athlete was assigned an individual support crew: Scott had Brenda, Put got my brother, Lori was blessed with Simon, and I my dad.

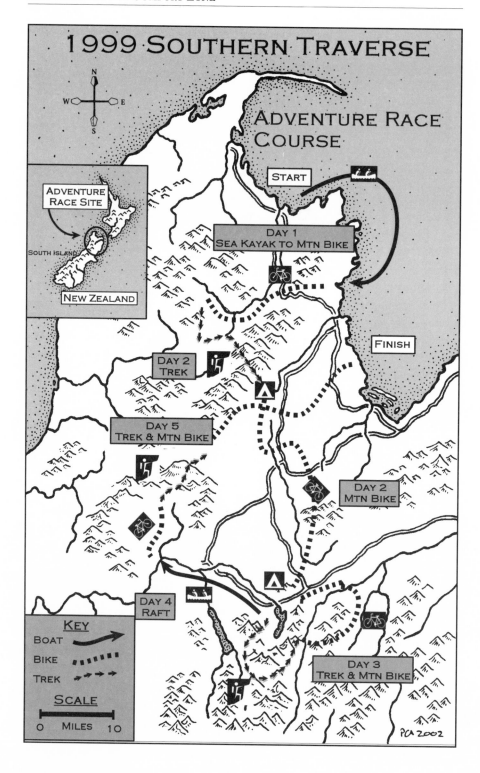

## Team Nomad's 1999 Southern Traverse Statistics
### (Times in Hours & Distance in Miles)

| Leg | Sport | Official Distance | Nomad's Distance | Nomad's Time* | Nomad's Cumulative Time | Cut off Total Time |
|---|---|---|---|---|---|---|
| 1 | Kayak | 25 | 25 | 7 | 7 | 10 |
| 2 | Bike | 34 | 34 | 11 | 18 | 18 |
| 3 | Trek | 16 | 16 | 24 | 42 | 33 |
| 4 | Bike | 63 | 63 | 12 | 54 | 50 |
| 5 | Trek | 25 | 20 | 26 | 80 | 72 |
| 6 | Bike | 25 | Leg Skipped | | 80 | 74 |
| 7 | Raft | 17 | 17 | 14 | 94 | 80 |
| 8 | Bike | 8 | Leg Skipped | | 94 | 83 |
| 9 | Trek | 8 | Leg Skipped | | 94 | 103 |
| 10 | Bike | 51 | 83 | 10 | 104 | 111 |

* Each time includes the time spent in transition. For example, it took six hours to kayak and one hour for transition, thus seven hours are reported for leg one's kayak time.

Total mileage of 275 is comparable to the distance from Boston to Philadelphia or nearly San Francisco to Los Angeles. The equivalent of 25 ascents and descents of the Empire State Building are part of the course.

At the start the next morning, the buzz of helicopters, TV crews and spectators jazzed up the multinational field. The gun went off and, in a flurry of paddles and a chorus of cheers, 200 competitors in 100 tandem sea kayaks shook off pre-race butterflies and headed seaward.

**BLUE SKIES AND WATERS AND A FOLLOWING WIND SUITED OUR TOUR OF ABLE TASMAN NATIONAL PARK. MOST TOURS TAKE THREE DAYS, WE TOOK SIX HOURS.**

In an effort to match the speed of our two tandem boats, Lori and I paddled in Put and Scott's wake. Regardless of the draft that sucked us along, I was hard pressed to keep up. My back and arms ached for four of the five hours we paddled. Mostly I passed the time worrying about sunburn, enjoying the scenery and exchanging competitive rancor with the other teams as we jockeyed around the points and beaches of Able Tasman National Park. We reached the beach at low tide, forcing us to drag the kayaks 200 yards across mud flats to the transition area. The lead teams were able to paddle to within 20 yards of shore on a high tide.

Our finish time of six hours placed us four hours ahead of the race official's maximum allowed time in 37th (of 50 teams) place (see chart). It had been me who had slowed the team on this leg. I thought it best to have been the weak link because it played directly to my instinct to push to the limit. However, being the weak link didn't teach me anything that might aid our team when the tables turned on the next leg.

A navigation clipboard had been mounted to my handlebars, making me the de facto orienteer for the mountain bike legs. In addition to his reconnoiter of the second mountain bike leg, my brother wrote out detailed directions for the roads and trails of the first mountain bike leg, which lead 34 miles over two 3,000-foot mountains. We checked out with the race officials and commenced what we expected to be a six-hour bike ride. In the first hour, my adrenaline was high as we jockeyed with other teams for position and got nearly immediate feedback on our route-finding decisions.

However, it was on this leg that the relative strength of each team member and such strength's effect on pace and morale emerged. Put and I rode up the hills that Scott and Lori were forced to walk. Lori's shoulders bruised from her oversized pack and it took two stops to remedy her problem.

At times, I could barely contain my impatience with our pace. Put and I surged ahead. If it weren't for passing support crew cars from other teams reminding us of the 100-meter maximum distance between team members rule, we might have been disqualified. In adventure racing, the theory is to test not only the physical and technical skills of individuals, but to force them

**HALF WAY UP TAKAKA PASS WITH TASMAN BAY IN THE DISTANCE, PUT HAD HARDLY BROKEN A SWEAT.**

to work as a unit under competitive and adverse conditions. The 100-meter maximum separation rule was intended to force teams to stay together. This tended to be especially difficult on the mountain bike legs.

Most adventure racing teams shift loads to stronger members immediately when pace differences emerge. An extreme example of this is short-roping slower bikers to stronger riders. Teams who did this were out to finish competitively. This was not the spirit we enjoyed, for we felt it demeaning.

We discussed load shifting, but the "it's just a little further to the downhill" face-saving excuse prevailed. In my case, I was reluctant to ask for the load out of concern for the laggard's feelings. Since we thought ourselves to be progressing at a reasonable pace on this the second leg, none of us felt compelled to call for shifting. I also perceived that if we did the race without load shifting, then each person could say to himself that he or she was able to complete it essentially solo. Since we were never out to be competitive in the race, we could afford this egalitarian rationale.

By the end of the mountain bike leg and the transition checkpoint where our support crew waited, our team's pace differences and attendant tensions faded. We had been on course 17 hours and would depart an hour later, exactly at the race organizer's cut off time—still on pace to finish the full course. The team spirit galvanized as we knew the next sport—mountain hiking was one of our strengths.

SIMON MIDDLEMASS (LEFT), A CHRISTCHURCH, NEW ZEALAND, CLIMBING GUIDE ADDED CHEER AND MATURITY AS LORI'S SUPPORT CREW.

We departed the transition zone and commenced the 1,000-foot climb to the table lands of Kahurangi National Park. Sixteen miles long, this leg would climb 5,500 feet and descend 6,500 feet. By comparison, a traverse of the Presidential Range in New Hampshire's White Mountains is 20 miles long through 17,000 vertical feet. A typical 14,000-foot peak in Colorado ascends and descends through 10 miles and 8,000 vertical feet. I didn't expect this leg to be too difficult.

Lori set a fast pace as her strength tended to foot travel. Put, I and Scott, respectively, followed her lead. By the end of the first climb, Scott dropped about 10 minutes behind. Suffering anaerobically trying to catch us—a mistake in a five-day race—Scott rightfully chastised us.

While we waited for Scott above treeline, I regretted not checking our self-serving surge, for I knew Scott was off pace. I thought, "We should, and by the race rules, stay together. Should we have taken some of his load, or just slowed down?" This judgement call was nearly impossible to make because we were not out to win, just to finish. Furthermore, the foot leg was supposed to be one of Scott's stronger suits. I knew that Lori's recent pace and my tenor since the beginning of the previous mountain bike leg suggested a pace indicative of a team out for a competitive finish. So, there it was, my actions were inconsistent with the stated goal of the team.

I feared my self-serving actions and our behavior would damage our team spirit and probably hurt Scott's feelings. Here was the second leg where he had been the weak link, and I was concerned he might not be having the fun he expected.

Rising above our insubordination, Scott assumed the lead and kept our pace rightfully in check. At about 2am and six miles into the traverse, Put acknowledged intermittent and debilitating gastrointestinal pain. A mile or so later we stopped to sleep for an hour in a trailside hut hoping Put would feel better. There, Put used our only sleeping bag. Scott and I separately sandwiched ourselves between two mattresses. Lori, who had been cold while hiking even with all of her clothes on couldn't stay warm. The simple solution would have been to nestle her between Scott and me, but gender-induced apprehension and lingering tension from the pace and other problems kept us separate. Lori suffered.

Put's condition was worse after an hour's rest. Yet, he continued racing—internalizing his near-constant stomach pain. Had I been in his place, I too would have continued stoically, rather than drop out so soon and dash the team's hopes for a ranked finish. Put had heavily invested his time, money and expectations in this race.

We all speculated on what could cause Put to be so ill. The easy answer was dehydration, but since Put had matched my fluid intake over the race so far, I knew his problem's cause lay elsewhere.

The next hours felt surreal. In the hours before sunrise, we climbed through foggy and windy forest sections, out onto tussocky slopes, and finally up onto rocky slopes dominated by bizarre karst (limestone) topography. The fog and clouds lifted at sunrise revealing a color-filled landscape. The colors ranged from the turquoise of the nearby Tasman Sea to the green slopes of forest that transitioned to the golden hues of the tundra tussocks across which we walked. Ahead were exposed limestone ridges and summits. The distance from valley floor to ridge line in this section of New Zealand's South Island was approximately 5,000 feet, or one mile.

Our nearly-silent march across the ridge line was suddenly interrupted by a helicopter. With cameras pointing out its door, it made a series of passes coming

AT SUNRISE ON DAY TWO, SCOTT BERK LEADS US THROUGH KAHURANGI NATIONAL PARK, OUR SECOND NATIONAL PARK IN LESS THAN 24 HOURS. ADVENTURE RACING, WHILE CONTRIVED, ENABLED ME TO SEE MORE OF NEW ZEALAND IN FIVE DAYS THAN MOST WOULD SEE IN FIVE WEEKS.

within 30 yards. It landed at the summit and filmed our approach. A TV commentator waited to interview us. My vanity sought an interview. But, as I thought about what I'd say if I got interviewed, the reality was we were experiencing things far too complex to communicate in a TV sound-bite.

That morning, I lagged behind the team until my internal clock allowed me to awaken. I don't think I slowed the team down, but some of the hills hurt. Scott was confused once by the terrain. He wanted to descend one valley too soon, a map-reading mistake that would have caused us hours to correct. I asserted my map reading opinion to avoid what I considered would be a disastrous choice. While Lori seemed unaffected by the exertion of this leg, she was challenged on steep and exposed sections. Put's gastrointestinal ailment had reduced his pace to five minutes of slow walking punctuated by down-on-all-fours retching after which he curled up on the ground.

**TRANQUILITY INTERRUPTED OR FORTUITOUS SALVATION? STEVE PUTNAM HOURS BEFORE RESCUE BY THIS HELICOPTER.**

I had never seen Put suffer so much in the 20 years I had known him. Convening a short distance from the helicopter, Scott set an objective for the team to reach the Ellis Hut check point, (a mile further and 2,000 vertical feet below us) where Put's condition would be evaluated. Before we moved though, I suggested that we consider asking for an evacuation for Put right then. That option was rejected, for we all agreed we were willing to risk temporarily slow progress in hopes of having our full team finish the course together. I went along with this tactic, but became more and more frustrated as other teams passed us like we were standing still and Put's condition rapidly deteriorated.

At Ellis Hut, the last check point before a four-mile forested trek to the next transition to mountain bikes, radio consultations with the race doctors directed Put to take 10mg of codeine-based pain killer from our first aid kit and rest for an hour. Despite a raft of questions about Put's symptoms, no one could pinpoint the cause of his malady. I could see disappointment mixed with pain on Put's face as we discussed our options if this remedy didn't work. Helicopter rescue was a decisive admission of failure, but one that would preserve some team options by letting the rest of us continue at a faster pace. It might have soothed Put's ego if he were to walk out, but, in his condition, the time it would have taken would have knocked us out of the race completely. Regardless of our mode and pace of egress, Put would be highly unlikely to complete the next leg.

While waiting the hour to see if the pain killer would work, Scott, Lori and I commiserated together momentarily and then retreated to our private

A STOMACH BUG TAKES DOWN OUR STRONGEST TEAM MEMBER. PUT (RIGHT) SUFFERED FOR 10 HOURS BEFORE RELUCTANTLY ACCEPTING HELICOPTER RESCUE. THE AUTHOR DIGESTS THE CONSEQUENCES.

thoughts. Our six-month plan was breaking down as we spoke. I was worried about Put's health, and believed strongly that he should be flown out. He was a liability to us if he were to hike any further. That was the reality and we were facing it. I had no problem with continuing on as a three-person team.

Like my first attempt on El Capitan, a pattern of failure in team events was appearing. I saw the value of team events as a shared experience with the possibility to achieve something greater than you could on your own. Ideally it should be done with lifelong friends so the experience can be relived at reunions. It was for these reasons that doing the race with Scott, Put, my brother and dad meant so much to me. Doing this event meant compromising one standard of mine—excelling at my highest level so that I could achieve another—the chance to complete the challenge of a multi-sport, multi-day team wilderness competition.

An hour later, Put got out of the bunk and tried to walk. He failed to make it more than 100 feet before he sat down and got sick for the fifth time that day. A chopper arrived an hour later, leaving Scott, Lori and me to hike four miles down 4,000 vertical feet through temperate rainforest.

It took us five hours to hike the four miles Put flew over in five minutes. The trail was hacked out of the rain forest into sides of a ravine. Nine times it descended 100 to 200 vertical yards to river level, crossed and reascended only to traverse for a few hundred yards and start the process again. The worst sections compared to walking on a greased, 45-degree-inclined garden trellis. At our limits of endurance and no longer fueled by the adrenaline of race incentives, our coordination and motivation were tested.

**PUT'S FINAL STEPS.**

Lori slipped while descending a near-vertical section of trail and grabbed a tree that left her suspended out over the slope. Scott maneuvered under her and pushed her back in so she could regain her footing. The pace of our team here was below what I could have done on my own, but I was resigned to our reality by now. The *"grovel"* part of our team motto applied here.

Once down to the mountain bike transition point, Scott convened our athletes and support crew to discuss options. Reports trickled in of five teams dropping out on the previous leg. It had been brutal for others too. I felt good enough to continue right away if necessary. Put was still suffering too much to resume. Lori opted out as she realized her expectations for the race differed substantially from its reality. I didn't try to change her mind, but inside I felt like she was copping out. It must have been disappointing for her that she wasn't having fun right now, but in my mind, being out of a comfort zone was part of the process of this race.

While sorting out Put's malady, we slipped into third-to-last place, five hours slower than maximum allowable time. To stay on the full course we needed to continue right away and make up our deficit before the beginning of the rafting leg—four legs hence where slow teams were diverted to an alternative and abbreviated course. The race organizers wanted to concentrate finish times to a 24-hour window.

With Lori and Put out, we were below the legal number of team members (three) to continue. My brother offered to ride the next leg, giving us hope that Put would recover or that Lori would change her mind and we could continue as an unranked, three-member team after this leg. So far out of contention, we didn't advise the race officials of our use of a stand-in. My brother's stand-in for Put didn't trigger any ethical debate for I believed that our rule-stretching wouldn't threaten any other team's experience and now, knowing we could not have a ranked finish, I just wanted to prove I could get around the course. I remembered my motto from El Capitan: Success over style. I wanted to finish what I came to do, despite stretching the rules.

Our plan settled, Scott opted for two hours of sleep before departure. He was so fatigued from the nonstop exertion of the last 36 hours, he feared that if he pressed on immediately he would not make it at all.

Our 10pm restart on mountain bikes brought on an unforgiving series of events. Within the first mile we had to ford a chilling,

THE AUTHOR, SCOTT AND LORI AFTER THE TOUGHEST TRAIL THE AUTHOR HAD EVER HIKED. MANY TEAMS QUIT AFTER THIS LEG. LORI CALLED IT QUITS MOMENTS AFTER THIS IMAGE WAS TAKEN, PUTTING TEAM NOMAD OUT OF THE COMPETITION.

waist-deep river to avoid a 10-mile detour. During the first two hours our speeds matched and we rode along at what I considered a good race pace, but as we moved into the third hour we encountered a relentless series of 1,000-foot, sweat-drenched climbs and freezing descents in a maze of overgrown and confusing logging roads.

My brother and I rarely hesitated as we settled in to grind to the top of the next hill. But each time we waited for Scott, it took longer and longer for his headlamp to appear. He barely spoke when he joined us and could barely catch his breath. We took half of his load. Steve and I slowed down, but soon we were going as slow as we could without walking on hills that just weren't that steep. My brother and I rode on in silence. We passed another team sleeping in a ditch. My competitive instinct drove me on as I realized that our pace was gaining us ground.

My instinct was to push onward, but reality linked my success to my team's performance once again. Scott, done-in by the pace and length of the race, was pushed nearly to his limit by the rise and fall of the terrain and his body temperature. We descended another hill into yet another cold valley. Another 1,000-foot climb awaited. Scott continued to lag. We had a problem. My brother and I never discussed what was becoming apparent—that Scott wouldn't make it or that we would be fated to crawl to the end of this next leg at a pace far below what we could have done on our own. He and I alternatively reminded each other to slow down so Scott could keep up. At the time there was nothing else we could do save pull Scott along and we didn't believe that would actually do us any good seeing that it was dangerous, we had 35 miles to go, and were done as a team if we slowed from our pace anyway (due to the ever-present cut off time).

The next thigh-deep river crossing came four hours into this leg—43 hours into the race. It quenched Scott's last spark. He weaved another hundred yards to the intersection of our logging road and a paved road where we waited. Marginally coherent, exhausted and cold, he said he was incapable of completing the final miles of this leg under his own power. He needed twenty-four hours rest and ample food, not just more load shifted to us or a further slowing of the pace.

Scott didn't agonize this decision. He indicated we were to continue without him. He changed to dry clothes, crawled into a sleeping bag and we wrapped him burrito-like in the tarp we had been required to carry. He handed me our team's emergency beacon. I quietly packed it away, for this transfer of the symbol of power might have been hard for Scott to swallow. Ironically, I was now leader of a team who was out of the race—just following the preset course to see if I could do it.

At the next check point, we put in a radio call to dispatch my dad and Put to pick up Scott. Steve and I cranked up to race pace again and rode through the rest of the night and into the morning, recording the second-fastest time of any team on this leg.

However, I was somewhat delirious by the end of this leg. I had been exercising for 48 hours on less than three-hours sleep. When my brother finished five minutes before me, I felt mildly angry at him for leaving me. I obviously couldn't swallow my own medicine.

With our fast arrival at the Nelson Lakes National Park transition zone where all of the teams' support crews camped out awaiting their athletes, we had gained six hours on the field and had advanced to one hour ahead of the cutoff time. Regardless, we were down to one team member and the race official disqualified us.

My dad wheeled my bike towards our support vehicles, I walked beside. I exhausted myself keeping up with my brother and my instinct to push to the limit. I saw tears of pride in my dad's eyes. One son had gone the furthest of the team and the other had, off-the-couch, carried the team's hopes. On the surface it looked like we all could go home satisfied.

AS TEAM DOCTOR AND STAND-IN ATHLETE, STEVE GENEREAUX (RIGHT) SET A HIGH STANDARD AND KEPT OUR TEAM VIABLE.

But then, from the direction of the other teams' camps, Scott and Brenda approached. They wanted to know if I could keep going. I said, "Possibly." They walked off, headed straight for one camp in particular.

Returning to where I was eating and gathering my wits, they said, "Bruce, we found a team whose captain got sick. They are willing to take you on." Brenda and Scott had sold my strengths to Team Hastings, a group of experienced, semiprofessional adventure racers.

THE AUTHOR AND HIS DAD SORT THINGS OUT AT A TRANSITION ZONE.

At first I thought: *"Here is a chance to get pulled up to a higher level and finish the course. I hope I can keep up. What do I have to lose?"* What I should have thought was: *"Three of them could have continued legally without me, why take me along—I just add one more reason for failure?"* Playing this sport by its rules had already proven that odds of failure were directly related to number of team members. What had Scott and Brenda really promised? Or were they in need of some help? Like El Capitan—it was unclear why they wanted me to come along.

In a state of physical exhaustion, I was forced to decide between the easy option of crawling into a tent for much-needed sleep and giving up on the race with everyone saying I did well, or joining unknown racers and trying to go further along the course, with the chance of finishing. I walked to the perimeter of their camp and eyed them. They looked like they had their act together except for the weeping blisters I spied on one guy's feet, an ominous sign only halfway through a five-day adventure race. Regardless, here was a chance to get around this course by hook or by crook.

Even in my sleep-deprived mental fog I knew there was no downside to continuing, only a fortuitous chance to push beyond my comfort zone once again. Figuring I'd regret it if I said "No", I announced I would continue. Last thing I saw as I ducked into a tent was my brother doctoring the blistered feet of my new teammate.

Roused a few minutes before our scheduled 3pm departure, I struggled back to consciousness and joined Scott and my brother to study the map. They reported that the fastest team had done this leg in 24 hours, which, based on our previous foot performance, indicated I was in for more or less a 36-hour hike, depending on the speed of my new teammates. To meet

BLAIN REEVES SHOWS THE ROUTE CHOSEN TO THE AUTHOR AS HE JOINS THE TEAM. AT LEFT IS THE INJURED CAPTAIN OF TEAM HASTINGS. AT RIGHT, MARGO DOWNEY OBSCURES DAN O'SHEA.

the minimum time to stay on the full course, however, we had only a 26-hour window—a daunting prospect. I wondered just how fast this team would be and how tough the leg would be.

The leg was to cover 10,000 vertical feet, cross two major ranges, traverse snow fields through glacially-carved horns and aretes and included a rappel off a 200-foot cliff. I gathered food and gear and joined my new teammates: Dan O'Shea, a Navy Seal; Blaine Reeves, a Captain in the U.S. Army Rangers; and Margo Downey, a professional adventure racer.

My new team led me out of camp towards the trailhead for the St. Arnaud Range of Nelson Lakes National Park. They opted for the most sure trail to the next check point. This took us on a slightly-circuitous route around the lake. Within a few hundred yards of leaving camp I saw a shorter path from camp to the trailhead. Unable to control my "back-seat driving" instinct even with people I had just met, I interjected my opinion. They agreed to my path, which fortunately saved us hundreds of yards and temporarily satisfied my instinctive desire for control. I followed them up the trail, a happy team member.

Blaine, my new team's designated navigator, resumed leading, carefully metering our pace over the next six hours. I gave what I considered reasonable suggestions to ensure the well-being of the group—such as taking off our boots for a knee-deep river crossing to avoid a foolhardy shoe-soaking. I also noticed that no one seemed to be pushing the pace. Maybe it was that the pace was already a push. But given our need to make up substantial amounts time, I felt we should take a chance and push our pace much faster.

The weather turned sharply colder as we ascended a series of near vertical rock headwalls below the checkpoint. We arrived at 10pm, glad for shelter and learned our pace had not gained us any ground towards meeting the cutoff time. This was sobering. Between us and the next transition zone to mountain bikes, lay glacial basins and ridges and summit crags so rugged that I suspected we would be very hard pressed to simply maintain pace, let alone move up. Not a minute could be spared. Sleep was not optional, it was out of the question.

On the approach hike to the hut, I learned that my new teammates were determined to finish the full course and felt their pace would accomplish this goal. Before the race and during the first two legs, they harbored hopes of a top-ten finish. Their abilities to find sponsors and teammates for future races depended on their results. This standard remained in place even though we were nearly in last place and weren't doing any catching up.

Having changed into warmer clothes and prepared our helmets, headlamps and rappelling harnesses, we left the St. Arnaud hut at 11:30pm and entered an eery blackness. The weather had deteriorated to periods of fog,

**MARGO DOWNEY CROSSES THE RIVER AT THE HEAD OF LAKE ROTOITI. THE SCENERY WAS AS GRAND AS OUR PLANS, BUT MICRO-MANAGEMENT AND INJURIES WOULD DOOM OUR EFFORT TO COMPLETE THE COURSE.**

snow squalls and broken clouds through which the moon peeked. The wind blew relentlessly, forcing us to raise our hoods up over our helmets, making it more difficult to communicate. The narrow beams cast by our headlights would soon mimic the narrowness of our perspectives as we forced our way through terrain and conditions that would test all of us.

Within yards of the hut we lost the trail and were forced to continue cross country, southward along the flank of a glacially-carved peak towards a sometimes-visible pass, one mile beyond which lay the mandatory 200-foot rappel. We traversed wet, rocky slabs and expanses of basketball-sized loose scree. Our pace was excruciatingly slow because our leader yielded to repeated requests for map micro-management by other teammates, resulting in second-guessed decisions at every terrain change.

My teammates tended to avoid any steep slopes in fear of getting cliffed, a risk-adverse tactic that caused us to travel a more circuitous route. Without a captain there was no clear leadership and coincident assumption of responsibility for decisions, good or bad.

My intuitive mountain sense and self-professed "internal GPS" tended to make my suggestions seem baseless, cavalier and risk-loving to them. I disregarded common orienteering practices such as back sighting and plotting courses and relied on moonlight-aided dead reckoning. We were above treeline in an obvious valley with fog and clouds only periodically obscuring landmarks. I felt it inappropriate to assert myself for my route changes would have had a minimal impact on our overall pace as it was the terrain, not our path through it that was constraining our pace. But, in this case I was neither a *de jure* or *de facto* leader. My success was once again limited by the ability of my teammates.

Compounding the discouragement induced by our route-finding frustrations, Blaine bullied through the scree sections, indifferent to the scree's ability to further damage his already blistered feet. He allowed that he was an Army Ranger, accustomed to leading men in the field. He was clad in lightweight, custom adventure-racing shoes that disserved his scree-walking technique and eventually served as blood reservoirs.

Traversing a slope of scree, marginally stable at its angle of repose, I found Margo slipping out of the character I observed on the approach to the hut. Then she had talked and walked at race pace. I was impressed by her fitness. She had an impressive list of adventure race results under her belt and expected her team to place in this race. Things hadn't gone so well so far with her captain dropping out, but she, Dan and Blaine were determined to get back on track. Given that they had never met before this race, I was impressed with how well they performed as a team. They seemed to be doing things by the same book.

However, on the loose scree slope, I learned that their apparent book-learning hadn't paid off, as their actual technical experience appeared limited when practiced under harsh conditions. Here were people being pushed beyond their comfort zone, and actions spoke louder than the words I heard earlier. Margo's pace slowed to the point where she contemplated each foot placement. Step by agonizing step, I supported her from below.

After the scree dancing episode, we clambered up ledges and crossed the divide into the shadowy northern head of a deeply-incised glacial valley. The terrain seemed to drop away in a black void. Clouds obscured the moon. I had no idea what to expect, but I knew I wouldn't let myself step off anything dangerous. I was not rushed by the pace, so I was able to maintain steady and safe progress. Things were not as easy for my teammates.

We alternated rock climbing down ledges, clambering around house-sized boulders and descending snowfields. Sixty-four hours into the race, just before the rappel station, I looked up and saw Dan lose his footing on one of the snowfields, and start sliding rapidly. He was headed for the rocks at about 20 miles per hour.

Moments before, I blithely boot-skied down the snow just like I had skied countless other snowfields while playing in the mountains on my own terms. Had I remembered my teammate's weaknesses over the past few hours, I might not have assumed my partners were as capable in the conditions as I.

Dan crumpled, feet first into the scree.

"Dan, are you OK?" I called over.

"Yeah, I am fine. It was nothing," he said brusquely, rapidly getting to his feet. I couldn't believe it. Either he was insanely lucky or masked his pain well. He couldn't have fallen so far and so fast and not sustained some kind of injury. I was relieved that he was not hurt as self-rescue at our level of fatigue would have been very difficult.

We approached the rappel station. Snow swirled and the wind gusted, drowning parts of every sentence. Muddy and wet fixed ropes led us down a series of wet and grassy cliffs to the edge of the rappel cliff where we stood, jackets crusting over with a muddy rime. Margo said all along she was afraid of heights and asked that I rappel beside her on the parallel ropes.

"Margo, first, clip your backpack to your harness between your legs and focus on letting the rope feed smoothly," I instructed. Her prussic knot back up should hold on a dry rope, but now the saturated rope we descended was frozen stiff like a wire. I could see a tense expression form on her face and her movements become less fluid as she fed the rope through her rappel device. Yet she never once lost control. On the ground she was all business again.

As we descended further down the glacial cirque through a two-city-block-sized screefield below, my coordination deteriorated. Like during the early hours of the two previous mornings, I succumbed to the effects of sleep deprivation. Despite

**A 200-FOOT RAPPEL ON THREE HOURS' SLEEP. FOR THE SECOND TIME THAT NIGHT, MARGO STEPPED TEMPORARILY OUT OF HER COMFORT ZONE.**

walking as slowly as possible, I still moved ahead of the rest of the team. I sat down to wait. To my right I saw lichen growing in a pattern on a black rock. I stared, zombie-like, at the rock and swooned towards sleep. Determined to stay awake, I focused in on the lichen, which suddenly morphed into the Road Runner being caught by Wiley E. Coyote.

Margo's approach broke my trance. I shook the parallel reality from my head and stood up. "We have to find the next hut and sleep an hour. According to the map it is right below this scree in the woods," I said.

She and I moved on, scouting for the hut. A few minutes of uncoordinated scree stumbling later, I saw a trailer-sized boulder move. Oddly it made no noise.

"There it is," Margo said, seemingly thinking for a moment that the same boulder was the hut.

In three days she had had one hour of sleep, and I three. I shared Margo's determination to maintain a full-course pace, but not a competitive finish. However, we were delirious with lack of sleep and Dan and Blaine were lagging. Sleep was necessary if we were to go on at all, regardless of the time issues. At 4:30am we finally staggered into the aptly-named Hopeless Creek hut. Dan helped Blaine in minutes later. Blaine's shoes were dark red in the heel areas and along the outside fronts. Bloodstained socks were pulled off and I saw the bandages my brother had set had worn through, revealing purplish/blue bruises encircling grossly-swollen, quarter-inch thick, tomato slice-like wounds. I was impressed that anyone could have endured that and kept walking.

Margo had been studying the map. She said something to the effect of, "We have 12 miles still to go, down 2,000 feet and then up 3,000 feet through one of those scree landslides to where the mountain bikes have been left. If we leave right now there is an outside chance we'll make it to the rafting under the cut off time. Come on guys, I came down here to place in this race and we are falling apart."

Dan said he'd need time to dress Blaine's feet. Dan's Navy Seal training qualified him to be our medic. I offered some of my codeine-based painkillers—the only thing I could add to supplement Dan's ministering, only to be rebuffed. Blaine thought his feet would be OK. I was too sleepy to call him on what I thought was a masochistic veil over reality. In retrospect, my comments wouldn't have changed his mind, for with Blaine instinct prevailed over reason.

Margo reiterated her expectation that we keep racing. Dan seemed to have lost his drive. We agreed to take one hour and then hit the trail. I pulled my sleeping bag out and climbed into an upper bunk. I was near my limit of being able to function without sleep.

Surprisingly, I couldn't fall asleep right away. My thoughts came in bursts. My determination to complete the course with minimal regret compelled me to accept an offer to team up with unknowns who proved to be the type of partners that I might not have otherwise chosen outside of a competition. Their backcountry experiences differed from mine. They spoke of military marches, set formulae for orienteering, and competition in other adventure races, while I remembered a river descended, a route climbed or a peak bagged with friends. Certainly they had experience pushing themselves and were mentally suited for this exercise, but the fundamental difference I saw between them and me was that I aspired to do the sports in this race for fun. To them it appeared that the sports were merely requisite parts to a greater whole—the adventure race.

They were a geographically diverse set of semiprofessional adventure racers. Owning their own gear and finding only a single sponsor, they teamed up through a mix of ability, chance availability and default. They had never trained together, yet expected to be competitive. Judging from the way they spoke of other races and racers and their single-minded determination, I was not surprised to learn that relationships had been damaged in previous races over performance and opinion differences.

I cared about finishing, not placing so I couldn't jump on Margo's racing-psychology bandwagon. I had no aspirations to make this sport a career, I just wanted to prove that I could complete this course. This adventure racing team seemed much like the typical corporate merger. It began with operational synergies to justify action, and then proceeded to claims of insurmountable chemistry and cultural differences as cause of failure. I was a rookie in the politics of adventure racing and it, like that media chopper two days before on Mt. Arthur, turned me off.

If there was a next adventure race for me, I would align myself with athletes whose abilities exceeded mine. That way I would be more likely to expand my comfort zone.

I was awakened by Blaine's convulsive shivering and babbling about bloody blisters. It was 6:30am, an hour after we should have left to stay on course. Margo was up and pacing the floor. I had trouble waking up, but once I grasped what was going on below, I knew there was no rush and that Margo's pacing was in vain.

Dan was trying to get going and talking nonstop about the myriad of things that had contributed to the team's downfall. He appeared depressed. Blaine was done and we all knew it. Margo persisted in berating the situation. There was palpable tension. For the second time in the race, my team was falling apart.

I couldn't care that much about their lost dreams of a competitive finish. I was disappointed that we couldn't push on, but understood the futility of trying to alter our reality. Margo and I talked about continuing on, but the wind was out of my sail. I was sympathetic to Blaine's debilitated feet. I believed that one shouldn't risk damage to his body when the goal of the event was clearly not going to be achieved, or the risk of an element beyond your control killing or injuring you was likely. This opinion kept me from pursuing high altitude mountaineering, but didn't prevent me from some kayaking that clearly presented unacceptable risks.

Despite Dan's patches, Blaine verged on tears as he pulled on his shoes. There was no option for us but to walk out, as Blaine weighed 200 pounds. Margo left the Hopeless Creek hut and set off down the trail alone, I presumed, in frustration. When I saw Blaine's knee-buckling, involuntary reaction to the pain of each step, I knew it would be hours before we caught Margo. I turned at the door of the hut and photographed the name, capturing the correlation between the hut's name and our chances in the race.

**THE SIGN ON THE DOOR TO THE HUT WHERE OUR FATE WAS SEALED.**

By the time we descended to the valley floor, Blaine was limping pitifully with each step. We found Margo waiting trailside, still fuming over our breakdown and talking about continuing on the course. She and I briefly contemplated continuing on up the scree without Dan and Blaine. After I said I wouldn't, she agreed reluctantly to hike out the direct way. I was out of food and my heel had developed a painful bruise, forcing me to walk only on the balls of my feet. I never had to test this limit. Margo, on the other hand, seemed to have no limits as she would have continued had I.

Blaine took two painkillers. I joined him, taking one, to ease my aching heel. The 2.5-hour hike went by fast. I enjoyed the company of Dan and Blaine. Margo sped ahead.

We arrived at the transition area at 3pm, four days into the race. Surprisingly, we were not disqualified for failing to complete the hiking leg and subsequent mountainbike leg. The race officials directed us to a shortened course—rafting and mountain biking only, eliminating the next mountain-hiking trek over an apparently treacherous and more relentless mountain called Mt. Owen.

Unranked and facing no time constraints, all competitive elements were removed and a new chemistry emerged. Scott Berk replaced Blaine, balancing a hybrid team—half Team Nomad and half Team Hastings.

Margo talked excitedly about the rafting despite the fact that she had never done it before. Scott was fired up to be back on course and I heard no more talk about pace or competitive finishes.

Minutes before the rafting start window closed, a raft and local guide became available. We scrambled to don wet suits, grabbed a huge bag of grub and set off down the Class 4 Buller River. I savored a can of beer after my dinner as we chatted and enjoyed the easy rapids at the beginning of our raft trip. Margo was a novice rafter, but proved to be as strong as any rookie I had seen. Both Scott and I took turns guiding the raft. Under my watch, we broadsided a rock, throwing Scott overboard. Lightening fast, the guide pulled him back in as he was pummeled over boulders in the shallow rapid, moments before he would have been run over by our raft. I was summarily relieved of my command.

We finished the raft trip at 9pm in a driving rain and were driven back to our camp where we opted to sleep, planning to start the final 83-mile "short course" mountainbike ride to the finish in the morning. There was no reason to press on in the night as we planned to enjoy our ride in the daylight.

The next morning, we rode briskly from the raft put-in through rolling farmlands and forests to the seaside resort finish. We lingered at checkpoints, visiting with race officials. While chatting with each other on long, flat sections, we found we were mostly evenly matched. Scott had recovered and enjoyed his chance to ride the distance. I savored the combination of a scenic ride with the challenges of route finding and occasional reminders that we were still in a race of sorts. It seemed as if Margo and Dan had accepted their team's dissolution and unfulfilled expectations. They relaxed their pace and tenor. It was as if I were on a weekend ride with friends.

I had energy to spare and took each hill as my personal challenge. I went just as fast as I could up each, at times moving minutes ahead of my teammates. Had I been on a mountain bike ride outside of this race I would have done the same thing. No frustration permeated my attitude, just bursts of private competition.

**TRANSITION TO RAFTING MARKED A SHIFT FROM COMPETITION TO CONTEMPLATION. OUR PACE RELAXED AND PEOPLE ENJOYED EACH OTHER'S COMPANY INSTEAD OF DANCING AROUND DIFFERENCES.**

It seemed fitting and respectful to the organizers that we finish together. We jockeyed for position as we approached, with each of us proving that we could move to the front. But when the line became visible, each of us backed off. Scott and I, had we not been balancing bikes might have grasped arms as we finished together. As one of the 20 finishers, our team completed a modified course in five days, some 30 hours behind the fastest team—a result about which I have no regrets. Cameras rolled, interviews went down. Dan jumped in the ocean, displaying his Navy Seal swimming talent. Scott and I drank beer with locals gathered to watch the finish. Margo talked with other competitors and officials. Finally our support crew arrived and we celebrated our finish again.

At the awards party the next night, Dan and Blaine indicated their desire to team up with me on future races. It was an enticing offer.

On the flight home, I finally figured out why I would subject myself to such a long-term physical ordeal. Instead of the split-second decisions and consequences of a Class 5 rapid or a free-solo of a rock pitch as a medium for getting fleeting rewards, the adventure race allowed minimal risk with a maximum chance to push my limits. Waiting at home was my new family, and challenges that would provide lasting rewards.

THE AUTHOR (STANDING) AND DAN
O'SHEA REACH THEIR RESPECTIVE ANGLES
OF REPOSE.

The author's "domestic adventure racing team," from left to right, top row: Si & Vicki Ford, Helen Schumann, Peter Genereaux, Steve Genereaux, Chet Warman, Jamie O'Connor, Sarah & Sam (hidden) Krimmel, the author, John Stoffel, Ford Kern Genereaux. From left-center, clockwise: Vinnia the cat, Hanna Jovine, Hans Silas Jovine, Heather Allison, Liam O'Connor-Genereaux, Sugar Genereaux, Olivia Jovine, Caleb O'Connor-Genereaux, Mairead O'Connor-Genereaux, Janna Ford Genereaux and Allison Tyndall Genereaux.

# Acknowledgments

## HELP ON THE WAY/SLIPNOT

I took inspiration from works of David Roberts, from which I learned something about the historical context of adventure genré writing. In the acknowledgments in his 2000 book, *Escape Routes*, Roberts also clued me in to the relationship between writer and editor with lines such as, "At its most uncomfortable, the exchange begins to resemble some court room drama, as the prosecuting editor rattles off the crimes against the written word performed by the quivering hack in the dock, during one of his more thoughtless sprees of verbal mayhem." Dena Foltz, my editor, kept the stories and my self-esteem intact through my voluntary inquisition.

In his 1986 book, *Moments of Doubt*, Roberts clearly sets forth a challenge faced by mountaineering genré authors: "Take the reader beyond the description of the next piton placement and tell them what the character is thinking, why he is motivated and what it all means." I have tried to achieve this.

Various individuals played roles in the preparation of this book. First, my wife, Janna, gave me the financial freedom to take the time for this project and space in her studio to craft the words and images. She also read the chapters first and gave me unflinching feedback that many times lead me to answers to the question: *What are you trying to say with this chapter?* Without her, I would be off having more adventures and proving actuarial tables on extreme sports mortality.

The second person influential in shaping this book was Dwight Aspinwall. He is a fellow climber, kayaker and a tinkerer with things and ideas. It was he who articulated the "beyond the comfort zone" theme. And, it was he who both coined the phrase and actually still does "flex his risk muscles." Dwight's influences on the book ranged from the philosophy and tone of certain chapters to word choices in specific sentences.

Dena Foltz of Freestyle Creative in Whitefish, Montana edited my adventure tales to ensure consistent, paced and cogent chapters such that the stories could easily be packaged as a book. Dena also took professional risks in assisting with the promotion of this book.

Warren Witherell, founder of Burke Mountain Academy, where I spent two years of high school learning first hand about pushing my physical comfort zone, put a clarifying polish on the manuscript. Additionally, his comments on the tone of my commentary and articulation of the purpose of a book allowed me to further eliminate peripheral elements (beyond what Dena had already excised) and keep to the subject of the book: the adventure tales.

I valued the input from my mother, father, brother, sister-in-law, father-in-law and other relatives as they read various chapters, versions of the manuscript and looked at drafts of the cover. They helped with context, memories and presentation. Additionally, I consulted and received feedback from some of the people in the stories. Their comments resulted in changes that hopefully better match their and my perceptions of events. Other friends gave assistance from their positions as climbers, kayakers, skiers, graphic designers, computer jockey's, artists, English majors, lawyers, adventure racers, geographers, booksellers, writers, former headmasters, journalists, filmmakers, National Park Service engineers, advertizing consultants and photographers.

All uncredited photographs in this book are mine. Other images came from private collections and professional stocks. Private contributors include: Kenny Llewellyn, Catherine Hansford, John Hill, Brad Schildt, Rob Masinter, Steve Putnam, Brenda Berg, Peter Genereaux and Andy Zimet. Five professional photographers contributed: Torrey Carroll, Bob Perry, Jed Weingarten, Olaf Sööt and Glenn Randall. The underlying maps found throughout the book were drawn by Peter C. Allen, a Fairlee, Vermont-based artist. All map and image overlays were drafted by me.

The book was physically written in Foxboro, Massachusetts, at the Boyden Public Library and in Hanover, New Hampshire at Dartmouth College's Sandborn House and Berry Library. Thanks to Peter and Joyce in the Evans Map Room at Dartmouth College for their help. The staff at Gnomon Copy in Hanover—Shad, Andy, James and Kelly—were instrumental in getting reproductions of the manuscript out "yesterday" for review and were generous with their time and expertise as the project progressed.

This book was lain out in Adobe's PageMaker 6.5. The images were prepared with JASC's PaintShop Pro 7.0 and Adobe Photoshop software.

No one can quarrel with how a person observes or reacts to another's behavior. However, in this book, there are instances where dialog, thoughts and feelings are attributed to characters. If there are any errors of perception or interpretation, I apologize. Such is the risk of writing character-based descriptive narratives. My motivations to write a memoir of my experiences force their inclusion.

THE *AIGUILLE DE JOSH*, JOSHUA TREE NATIONAL PARK, CALIFORNIA, APRIL 1994. THE AUTHOR'S BULLY PULPIT MOVES FROM ROCK TO PAPER WITH THE PUBLICATION OF THIS BOOK.

# Reflections

FOLLOWING IS THE LONG VERSION OF THE INTRODUCTION THAT WAS PULLED FROM THE FRONT OF THE BOOK TO ENABLE THE READER TO IMMEDIATELY GET TO THE STORIES. I PUT THIS VERSION IN HERE BECAUSE THERE IS COMMENTARY THAT IS RELEVANT TO THE PRODUCTION AND PHILOSOPHY OF THE BOOK THAT I WANTED RECORDED.

*Beyond the Comfort Zone* is an autobiographical adventure narrative that strips away the veneer of elitism and ego while revealing what it feels like for an average athlete to extreme ski, rock climb, whitewater kayak and adventure race.

Dwight Aspinwall, a friend and fellow whitewater kayaker who can joke about even the most serious of subjects, read an early draft of this introduction and told me to lighten up. The seriousness of this book's treatment of near-death, disasters, dysfunctional relationships and motivations to accept risk made him uncomfortable. His reaction told me I had succeeded in my objective: to examine the motivations, thoughts and feelings of extreme sportsmen as they practice their craft.

I haven't written about summiting Everest or bickering over who will be on the summit team of some mountain whose name it seems everyone presumes you should know. This book is about me, a light-starch, white-collar professional by day and hobby adventurer by evening and weekend. I push the envelope a bit more with each chapter's adventure story.

However, my progression towards greater challenges is no different than what every other person on this planet experiences. As we age and add more complexity to our lives, sometimes we take risks that at first seem outlandish, but as we get acclimated, it becomes apparent that slightly more risk becomes acceptable. I write about those who voluntarily take risks during their leisure, not about the salt-of-the-earth who, by default of their geographic, socioeconomic or other circumstances take physical risks everyday to put food on the table. I, and presumably most readers of this book, fall into the category of recreational risk-takers who have never had to worry about starting over upon failure of a venture. For the reader of this book then, the sports I chose are a medium to address risk-taking by those who choose to do so because they want to, not because they need to.

My goal was to publish a series of stories written the way I wanted them so that my perspective on life's evolution could be told. As I did this I also attempted to make the subject accessible to the lay reader by weaving parallel contexts of typical lives—school, work, relationships and friends—into the fabric of stories that tell of progressively more risky behavior outdoors. The result hopefully is that the reader may simply live vicariously through these narratives or may extend his involvement to ask of him or herself what they would have done in my situation. With photographs, maps and words combined to covey the drama of the situations you will read about, your pulse should quicken as your psyche starts to create images of how and why we take risks in our lives.

As the manuscript for this book started to take form, I thought I would find material in my experiences from which to form a character development study—an aspect to the book thesis that I thought would differentiate it within the adventure narrative genré. But, what I found while reviewing my three decades of adventures was that my character did not change, it just repeatedly manifested itself. So, instead of a character development exposé as a criteria for choosing from my inventory of adventures, my selection task was simplified to the most compelling adventures and/or personally revealing experiences.

As I reflected and chose, the common theme seemed to be that I voluntarily stepped into the space beyond my comfort zone on my adventures. I realized that a portion of my self-actualization derived from regularly pushing limits. Blinded to the consequences of being drawn to this challenging space, I dredged up memories of how I rubbed people wrong along the way. The upshot of mixing my best adventures with this interpersonal dysfunction forced me to face up to those tensions in the stories. The chosen examples did not dodge the conflicts, nor were they revised as apologies, but they attempt to reflect an honest and entertaining rendering of a rich and varied life that I would not have changed. This personal-revelation theme enables the use of the word *confessions* in the book's subtitle.

As I barged forward with my project, I read David Roberts', 1986 book, *Moments of Doubt,* in which he suggests that "No mountaineer should write his autobiography before age forty." I held his opinion in such esteem that I feared failure. But then my ego kicked in and I thought, "I have always crammed as much into my life as I could," such that I believe I qualified early (this project started when I was 37, and as I write this introduction a few months before publication, I've reached age 39). Regardless of whether my life's experiences were sufficient to cut a few years from Roberts' timetable, the time was right for me to give it a try.

I was able to transfer my adventures to paper when I chose to forego corporate ambition for family. I weaned myself from pushing athletic limits that could get me killed, and sought more subtle satisfaction in my recreation. I no longer joked about trying to "drown myself" after a weekend kayaking trip for I no longer pushed myself so far as to trigger the analogy. A final constraint was removed when I became temporarily financially independent through sale of a house and my timely entry and reasonably-timed exit of the technology stock exuberance. This freed me from traditional work and, finding a highly-supportive partner in my wife, Janna, I threw myself headlong into a truly selfish project not normally an option for others at my age whose business is not writing.

In answer to the question often posed about my credentials to actually write an adventure narrative, I relate some of my relevant experience. After a privileged education and competitive sports life in New York and Vermont that culminated at ski racing academies in Vermont and Middlebury College, I moved to Colorado for graduate school at Colorado School of Mines. I grew to become a liberal arts adventurer and businessman. By "liberal arts" I mean my experience was a mile wide, but fairly shallow. I continued to dabble in ski racing, I became a 5.10 rock climber, Class 5 kayaker, an avid mountainbiker, an accomplished mountaineer and an occasional competitive distance runner. As a veteran of seven years business analysis work and two years as an executive for a mining company, I now feel as if my career "dragons" have been slain. I have applied my education, business writing experience and three decades worth of adventures to the production, writing and publishing of this book.

Some readers claim they remain dissatisfied even after an adventurer explains his motivations to accept risk of death as he pursues his sport. Below I attempt to describe the overriding determinant of my behavior as a contextual guide to the reader before the situation-specific motivations in each chapter are revealed.

My parents sacrificed time and money to make a myriad of outdoor sports available and the best education possible for my brother and me. Initially, we were encouraged, and then, as we aged, chose to squeeze in the next activity, rain or shine. While my brother and I were never quite the best, we always pushed and competed to get as far as we could. When we left home in our late teens, our characters had been formed such that pushing beyond our comfort zones was normal.

By weight of the success of my parent's generation to develop an economy that allowed reasonably-assured independence to the well educated, I never worried about my next roof or meal. I possessed a strong work ethic, committed to jobs through thick and thin and never shied away from hard work. Invariably, however, I found that even while I climbed as fast as I could up the corporate ladder and chased relationships all across town, I still had energy to burn. My outlet was to test myself in the crags and torrents of the world—all at standards considered risky by my peer group. Climbing, skiing and kayaking the hardest features I could find made me feel alive and complete.

Doubtless in any outdoor adventurer's motivation quiver is the reward he or she gets from being in the natural setting. As a geology major and lover of geography, I thrived on the unique views I got through my skiing, climbing, whitewater and adventure racing trips.

An aspect of human nature researched and aptly described by Joe Simpson in his book, *This Game of Ghosts,* called deep play resonates through my life. Simpson states: "The eighteenth century theologian and philosopher, Jeremy Bentham, developed a theory he called 'Deep Play,' whereby what the player stands to lose is completely disproportionate to what he can possibly gain."

When I was an impressionable youth, my paternal grandfather, Raymond P. Genereaux, told me stories of his childhood. He told of climbing Mt. St. Helens in 1917 when he was 15 years old. When I reported my ascent to him in 1986, five years after it erupted, his pride was evident, but he reminded me, part in jest, part in boast, that it was 1,300 feet higher when he summited. It was he who encouraged me to document my climbs and not be ashamed of my ego. I now maintain what I call my "recreational curriculum vita." This book happened in part because of this prompt.

Other parallels with my grandfather's life are significant to this book. My grandfather was smart, capable and controversial. As a lauded chemical engineer for the E. I. DuPont Company, his 39-year career notably included significant participation in the Manhattan Project and its spin-off projects in Hanford, Washington, whose results contributed to the end of the WWII and the advent of nuclear power. While stationed in Washington, he vacationed with his wife and children at a dude ranch adjacent to Mt. Rainier that, thanks in part to my grandfather's efforts, was designated by Congress the William O. Douglas Wilderness Area in 1985. This apparent philosophical inconsistency between what he did for his employer and what he did recreationally never appeared to bother him.

Before I began this book I worked as a mining executive. During the week, my job involved recommending to management which mine development project to fund. I was stationed in Denver, Phoenix and Sacramento—all outdoor recreational paradises. In essence, my mining job broadened my recreational experiences. I put 40,000 miles a year on my Jeep in a near-addictive mission every weekend, holiday and vacation to sample every mountain, canyon, cliff and river I could find.

I was introduced to the beauty of Chile's mountains and countryside through a business trip to investigate the opening of a mine in the Atacama Desert. I found it strangely fulfilling when I learned that a 1930 project of my grandfather's investigated the same technique for extracting copper now proposed for my Atacama project.

For all of the academic and business interest I professed on those trips to Chile, my eyes were always glued to the Andean Cordillera. Subsequently, I returned to Chile to explore its mountains and rivers solely for recreation. Like my grandfather, I embraced the beauty and wildness of my environment and paradoxically facilitated destruction of the same. I never felt I needed to forsake one for the other. I easily rationalized that the standard of living our society enjoyed required environmental sacrifice.

My grandfather's successes bolstered my confidence, for, through him I knew the ability to succeed was in my blood. In the fall of 1999, five months before his death, I dedicated my participation in an upcoming adventure race in New Zealand to him because I wished to honor the direction he gave my life.

*Bruce M. Genereaux,*
Hanover, New Hampshire
November 2002

HELEN MILLIKIN GENEREAUX AND RAYMOND PAUL GENEREAUX, WILMINGTON, DELAWARE 1987.

**LIKELY THE FIRST SKI DESCENT OF CASTLETON TOWER'S SCREE CONE. MAY 1989. DOES IT SURPRISE YOU NOW?**

# Index

Peter Genereaux

**Carving at Canyons, Utah.**

**DIVERSIONS WHILE PORTAGING ON THE SECOND DAY OF LOWER MILL CREEK, CALIFORNIA.**

**HOPE YOU FOUND WHAT YOU WERE LOOKING FOR. I SURE HAVE. FRESHIES ON SIGNAL PEAK, SIERRA NEVADA, NORTHERN CALIFORNIA. JANUARY 1999.**

CLASS FIVE PRESS
Six Ledyard Lane
Hanover NH 03755

CLASS FIVE PRESS
Six Ledyard Lane
Hanover NH 03755

PLEASE SEND TO: _____

_____ COPIES OF ***Beyond the Comfort Zone***

ADDRESS:

_____

_____

PHONE: _____

E-MAIL _____

**$20 FOR ONE**      **$35 FOR TWO**      **$100 FOR SIX**

INVOICE WILL ACCOMPANY SHIPMENT

ORDER BY E-MAIL AT ORDERS@CLASSFIVEPRESS.COM

FULL REFUND AVAILABLE FOR ANY REASON

---

PLEASE SEND TO: _____

_____ COPIES OF ***Beyond the Comfort Zone***

ADDRESS:

_____

_____

PHONE: _____

E-MAIL _____

**$20 FOR ONE**      **$35 FOR TWO**      **$100 FOR SIX**

INVOICE WILL ACCOMPANY SHIPMENT

ORDER BY E-MAIL AT ORDERS@CLASSFIVEPRESS.COM

FULL REFUND AVAILABLE FOR ANY REASON

CLASS FIVE PRESS
Six Ledyard Lane
Hanover NH 03755

CLASS FIVE PRESS
Six Ledyard Lane
Hanover NH 03755

PLEASE SEND TO: _____

_____ COPIES OF ***BEYOND THE COMFORT ZONE***

ADDRESS:

_____

_____

PHONE: _____

E-MAIL _____

**$20 FOR ONE     $35 FOR TWO     $100 FOR SIX**

INVOICE WILL ACCOMPANY SHIPMENT

ORDER BY E-MAIL AT ORDERS@CLASSFIVEPRESS.COM

FULL REFUND AVAILABLE FOR ANY REASON

---

PLEASE SEND TO: _____

_____ COPIES OF ***BEYOND THE COMFORT ZONE***

ADDRESS:

_____

_____

PHONE: _____

E-MAIL _____

**$20 FOR ONE     $35 FOR TWO     $100 FOR SIX**

INVOICE WILL ACCOMPANY SHIPMENT

ORDER BY E-MAIL AT ORDERS@CLASSFIVEPRESS.COM

FULL REFUND AVAILABLE FOR ANY REASON